The
Health & Safety Handbook

For Voluntary & Community Organisations

Second edition

Al Hinde and
Charlie Kavanagh
Editor *Jill Barlow*

Legislation updated by
Karen Cobham and
Laurie McMillan

Updated for reprint by
Laurie McMillan

DIRECTORY OF SOCIAL CHANGE

Community Health Advice & Training (CHAT) Project
Supported by the National Lottery Charities Board

Published by
The Directory of Social Change
24 Stephenson Way
London NW1 2DP
Tel: 020 7209 5151, fax: 020 7391 4804
e-mail: books@dsc.org.uk
from whom further copies and a full publications list are
available.

The Directory of Social Change is a Registered Charity
no. 800517

CHAT is a subsidiary of the Liverpool Occupational Health
Partnership
Registered Charity no. 1033189 and Company Limited by
Guarantee no. 2892625

First published 1998
Second edition published 2001
Reprinted 2003
Reprinted 2005

ISBN – 10 1 903991 01 3
ISBN – 13 978 1 903991 01 5

British Library Cataloguing in Publication Data
A catalogue record for this book is available from the British
Library

Text and cover designed by Linda Parker
Typeset by Linda Parker
Printed and bound by Page Bros, Norwich

Other Directory of Social Change departments in London:
Courses and conferences 020 7209 4949
Charity Centre 020 7209 1015
Charityfair 020 7391 4875
Publicity & Web Content 020 7391 4900
Policy & Reasearch 020 7391 4880

Directory of Social Change Northern Office:
Federation House, Hope Street, Liverpool L1 9BW
Courses and conferences 0151 708 0117
Policy & Research 0151 708 0136

Health @ Work

Health @ Work (formerly known as Liverpool Occupational Health Partnership) is an independent research and development organisation, striving to address and prevent health problems due to work. It has done some innovative work in general practices, facilitating general practice teams as organisations in their own right, to develop their own action plans to address health and safety, and informing patients about occupational health issues.

Health @ Work, Melbourne Buildings, 21 North John Street, Liverpool L2 5QU
Tel: 0151 236 6608; Fax: 0151 236 6625; E-mail: Danielle@healthatworkcentre.org
Website: www.healthatworkcentre.org.uk

Al Hinde

Al was employed by the Community Health Advice & Training (CHAT) Project when the first edition of the *Health & Safety Handbook* was written and published in 1998.

Al, a qualified mechanical engineer, has held various positions in health, safety and training with major UK companies and holds a diploma in health and safety, awarded by the National Examination Board for Occupational Safety and Health (NEBOSH).

Having been an active member of the Association of Lions Clubs International for 24 years, Al has considerable experience in various community-based activities encompassing welfare and fundraising. He has spent many years as a District Safety Officer for the Lions Clubs in the counties of Lancashire and Cumbria.

Charlie Kavanagh

Charlie has worked for Health @ Work since its conception in 1991. Charlie helped to develop the CHAT Project, which was funded by the National Lottery Charities Board and offered health and safety advice to voluntary and community groups, until the project finished in 2002.

He has extensive experience of the voluntary sector, and for four years was the Company Secretary of the Stephen Park Trust, which provided a countryside residential centre in rural Lancashire for use by schools and community groups in Merseyside. For five years, Charlie held the post of Secretary to the Liverpool & District Victims of Asbestos Support Group, which helps individuals affected by asbestos and their families.

Jill Barlow

Jill was the Manager of Liverpool Occupational Health Partnership. Both Jill and Charlie have written a range of articles on work-related health. Jill is a member of National Occupational Health Projects and the National Occupational Health Forum, and has an MSc in Health from Liverpool John Moores University.

Karen Cobham and Laurie McMillan

Karen and Laurie were employed by CHAT, and both have extensive experience of health and safety, especially in the voluntary sector. Laurie is currently employed by Health @ Work and has extensive experience of health and safety in many areas, especially in the voluntary sector. He is a member of the Institute of Occupational Safety & Health (IOSH).

Contents

By following the steps below, and completing all the stages, your organisation will be on the way to achieving the basic health and safety requirements needed to comply with current health and safety legislation and or duty of care.

About the voluntary sector

The voluntary sector is playing an ever more important role in society. Its size is increasing – estimates from workforce surveys indicate that it comprises almost 500,000 employees, and it has been suggested that over 20 million people a year do some form of voluntary work. Although most organisations are still relatively small and have incomes of less than £20,000, the sector as a whole has an annual income of around £14 billion.

Among the diverse range of voluntary organisations with radically different traditions and activities, there are plenty of examples of creativity and innovation in attempting to meet society's needs. Much of the good work achieved by the sector stems from the enthusiasm and commitment of the members of a group's governing body, and of its employees and volunteers, but laudable intentions alone are not always sufficient to produce an effective organisation.

Good management is crucial to organisations in the voluntary sector. This presents some with a moral dilemma – although it is appreciated that resources need to be managed efficiently, there may be an understandable reluctance to spend time or money on internal management rather than the organisation's main cause or purpose. However, this can be a false economy, particularly in the case of health and safety, for how can an organisation care for others when it does not care for itself?

It is vital that the management of health and safety in an organisation receives the same amount of attention that is given to other important issues such as the management of staff, financial controls, and the quality of service or product. Voluntary organisations can ill afford to wait until an accident occurs because of negligence, so opening the doors to potential fines and legal action.

Health and safety in the voluntary sector

There is a huge human and financial cost attached to accidents and ill health due to work in the UK – 187 million days are lost a year and the economy loses nearly £17 billion annually as a result. No separate figures are collected to quantify the number of accidents or incidence of ill health that have occurred in the voluntary sector but, given the scale of the problem, the size of the sector and several high-profile cases at the turn of the millennium, it is safe to assume that the sector has no room for complacency.

It is fair to say that health and safety law has not been written with the voluntary sector in mind. This has led to some areas of health and safety law affecting the sector being under-developed, which in turn has resulted in the legal responsibility placed on voluntary sector organisations being ill defined and confusing in some cases. However, we should never forget that health and safety legislation has led to an overwhelming reduction in accidents and illness in the UK and that it is designed to minimise the risk of injury to all people at work.

Complying with health and safety law is a positive process which can benefit both an organisation and the individuals – paid or unpaid – associated with it, by improving morale and by reducing staff/volunteer turnover and absenteeism. So it is clearly in everyone's interest to have good health and safety procedures and practices in place. Using this book will help you to reach this goal.

What about your organisation?

If your organisation employs paid staff, it will be treated as a small business by the enforcing authorities and you will have to meet health and safety legal requirements such as carrying out risk assessments, providing employers' liability insurance and meeting fire regulations. The definition of an employee is an individual working full or part time, doing manual, clerical or any other kind of work, who has a contract of employment. This applies whether the contract is written, or agreed verbally. Note that payment of some expenses may constitute an employment contract in some cases, so your organisation should make a clear distinction between employees and volunteers.

If your organisation has volunteers only, as a member of the governing body or the person in charge you still have a legal responsibility to your volunteers and members of the public. This responsibility is called duty of care, and under law you have a duty to protect volunteers and members of the public from hazards resulting from your organisation's activities.

This book has been written to meet the needs of all organisations, whether they employ staff, rely entirely on volunteers, or have a mixture of both.

We strongly recommend, on both a moral and a legal basis, that all organisations should attempt to implement all the health and safety requirements of the present law to cover all staff and volunteers. Organisations that pride themselves on their non-discriminatory practice would find it hard to justify offering different standards of health and safety to volunteers from those offered to paid staff. Surely it is a basic right to be assured of a safe environment in which to carry out voluntary work? Your organisation may not be able to meet every requirement of the law all at once, but writing out a health and safety policy and carrying out risk assessments will help you to prioritise areas of greatest need and set in motion an action plan for future improvements.

You should adopt this approach for several reasons, not least of which is that if an accident occurs, the action you have taken to reduce risk will go a long way to show that you are taking health and safety seriously. It will also help to protect your organisation's good name and may limit any future legal action by showing that you have attempted to comply with your duties towards those who are affected by your activities. Looking after the health and safety of your staff and volunteers is also a practical demonstration of the value that you attach to them.

We hope this book will help individual organisations to begin the process of improving their health and safety, thus protecting one of the most valuable assets of the voluntary sector – its people.

How to use this book

This book is a practical step-by-step guide to building up your health and safety policy. We advise that you read through the book first, and then complete the health and safety policy as you work through the book, filling in the checklist in appendix 1 as you go.

The policy should be as individual as your organisation – it is not something you can get off a shelf.

Don't forget that the policy is not set in stone, and needs to change as your organisation changes.

The book will also act as a source of reference for all your health and safety needs, covering current legislation. You need to be aware that health and safety legislation will change from time to time and you should incorporate any changes in relevant legislation into your policy.

Introduction

We have produced a guide to health and safety for the charity and voluntary sector which can be easily read and is accessible to all members of the sector. The new edition has been revised and updated to take acount of recent legislation. The forms included in the book have been revised and simplified, some of the text has been reordered, and a new section on stress has been added (see chapter 10).

The book is essential to the small organisation with only a handful of volunteers and an income of a few pounds, and also to the much larger organisation with many full-time employees and an annual income of millions.

Every voluntary organisation has a duty to ensure good standards of health and safety for its employees, volunteers, members of its governing body and the public. We often come across voluntary groups employing five or more staff that have a written safety policy (which is a legal requirement). However, only once have we come across a group that included volunteers in its policy. Invariably, these same groups quite rightly have equal opportunities policies in place, but fail to see that they are effectively discriminating against their volunteers by not including them in their health and safety policies. Even though an organisation has fewer legal obligations towards its volunteers compared with its employees, there is a strong moral case for applying the same health and safety standards to all people involved in an organisation's activities. We believe that grant-awarding bodies also have a moral responsibility to request evidence of satisfactory health and safety procedures – as they already do with equal opportunities policies.*

This book will help you to deal with health and safety in a simple and practical way. Although managing health and safety issues can be difficult, this book will give you clear guidelines on what to do, how to do it and who to consult. We have attempted to make the process as uncomplicated and as straightforward as possible, and we have used practical examples to clarify legal and technical points made. This is reflected, for example, in the new section on stress, where we have tried to help you on a practical level to tackle this complicated issue.

We believe the book will have been successful if it helps to improve attitudes towards managing health and safety in the voluntary sector. This should not be treated as a chore that can be completed and then forgotten. Rather, there must be an ongoing commitment to incorporate good health and safety standards into all of your organisation's activities. One of the underlying themes of recent health and safety legislation is assessing the risk of an accident occurring (whether this involves a person tripping and injuring themselves, or a fire breaking out and damaging property) and determining what action is required to prevent or reduce the chance of the accident happening. This process is called risk assessment. It does not always require experts to assess the hazards and risks in an organisation (although sources of specialist advice are available) – the people involved in the work are normally the ones who know it best. Using this book, an organisation can go a long way towards improving its own health and safety standards.

---

* A good example is the Netherley and Valley Partnership Community Development Fund in Liverpool, which asks all voluntary organisations applying for a grant to supply a copy of their health and safety policy. This has led several groups to look seriously at their health and safety procedures for the first time.

Authors' notes

1 This book has been produced to help those who have responsibility for the health and safety of voluntary and community organisations to comply with their legal responsibilities and/or duty of care.

2 In this book the term 'organisation' is used to include clubs, groups, social organisations, charity organisations, or any other non-profit-making organisation working in the voluntary sector.

3 The trustees of a charity are the people responsible under a charity's governing document for 'the general control and management of the administration of a charity'.[†] If your organisation is an unincorporated association, the charity's trustees will be members of the executive or management committee; if your organisation is a charitable company, the trustees are usually called the board of directors. For ease of reference and clarity, in this book we have used the term 'members of the governing body' for all people with legal responsibility for the administration and management of voluntary organisations.

4 If you are responsible for a voluntary organisation as a member of a governing body, then you and your fellow members have a shared responsibility to understand and control the hazards associated with the organisation's activities – even if the day-to-day responsibility is delegated to one individual, whether paid or unpaid.

5 All organisations, no matter how small they are, or how infrequently they meet or organise events, need to understand the health and safety legal requirements which are relevant to them. Ignorance of the need to comply with health and safety law or duty of care is not a defence in court.

6 Complying with health and safety responsibilities can sometimes be difficult, but by using this book as a guide you can begin to organise and manage your health and safety. It should not be used as a short cut to reach only the minimum standards, but as a stepping stone towards the improvement of health and safety in your organisation. A checklist is provided in appendix 1 for you to record your progress.

7 The information contained in this book is intended as a general guide based upon legislation at the time of going to press. Neither the sponsor, its staff nor the authors can accept liability for any loss arising as a result of reliance upon any information contained herein. Readers are strongly advised to obtain professional advice on an individual basis.

† *Charities Act 1993.*

Chapter 1
Duty of care

An important concept in health and safety is 'duty of care', which is a general legal duty on both individuals and organisations to avoid carelessly causing personal injury or damage to property. This is a duty in common law[1] which we all owe to our fellow human beings. For employers, this has been developed and extended by health and safety legislation. Details of basic legal requirements with regard to health and safety are outlined throughout the book.

Liability

If someone (the plaintiff) suffers injury, loss or damage because a person or persons (the defendant(s)) were negligent (at fault), the plaintiff can claim damages from the defendant(s) if they can prove negligence by showing that:

♦ they were owed a duty of care by the defendant;

♦ the duty of care was broken;

♦ the injury, loss or damage suffered by the plaintiff occurred as a result.

The standard is that of reasonable care and, generally, it can be said that the greater the risk, then the higher the standard of care which is required.

The part of the law covering damages (compensation) is civil law, which is concerned with the legal rights of the individual. There are legal requirements as to the types of insurance that must be held in order to cover certain compensation liabilities (for example, drivers must have third party insurance as a minimum – insurance is covered in more detail below, in chapter 4).

Organisations with employees

Employers have a statutory duty to take care of employees and others under statute law,[2] which is concerned with rights and wrongs in society. If they break their duty of care, they can be tried in a criminal court and, if found guilty, liable to pay a fine or, in serious cases, sent to prison.

'Employees' are individuals working full or part time, doing manual, clerical or any other kind of work, who have a contract of employment with the employer. This applies whether the contract is written, or agreed verbally.

In the event of an accident, an employer can be found to be criminally liable and ordered to pay a fine, as well as being civilly liable and obliged to pay damages. While organisations can insure against claims for damages through negligence, they cannot insure against the punishment and the payment of fines. Note also that employers have 'vicarious' liability for acts of negligence on the part of their employees, which means that an employer could be liable even if they did not authorise the employee's act or knew nothing about it.

Organisations with volunteers only

Organisations with volunteers only will not be held criminally liable under employment law, as they are not bound by these laws. However, they could be found criminally liable under other laws – for instance, if they own their premises or if they are the sole occupants, they could be found

---

1 Generally, the common law relates to non-statute law made as a result of judges' decisions in cases.

2 Statute relates to an act of Parliament; statute law is the body of enacted law or legislation together with the accompanying judicial decisions which explain individual statutes.

criminally negligent for breaking the duty associated with their occupancy (for example, see chapter 8 on fire procedures).

In general, for organisations with volunteers only, liability is based on the common law duty of care. If a volunteer is asked to carry out a task which results in them injuring themselves, the members of the governing body may be liable. For example, if a volunteer is injured while lifting a client out of a chair, the organisation could be found to be negligent if the volunteer had not been given suitable training in how to lift people, or if assistance was not available to help lift the client.

In this context, consideration will be given to the system of work. It might also be argued that voluntary organisations have not met their duty of care if they have failed to obtain and keep up-to-date with relevant literature. Employers are clearly under a duty to do this (keeping up-to-date with guidance from the Health and Safety Executive, for example), but the same may also be said of voluntary organisations.

Even if a volunteer has clearly been negligent, the members of the governing body could still be liable if they have not acted reasonably in training or supervising the volunteer. For example, if a volunteer drove a vehicle on the organisation's business and after an accident it was discovered that they did not have a full driving licence, the members of the governing body could be liable for not checking the volunteer's licence. The notion of duty of care needs to be considered in all aspects of an organisation's work and activities.

In the event of litigation (going to court), each case is decided individually on its merits and the particular circumstances, although case law (i.e. what has happened in similar cases before) may be referred to in evidence. The amount of effort that members of the governing body have put in to assessing the likelihood of certain events occurring, and the preventive action they have taken, will be relevant in deciding whether or not they have been reasonable (see chapter 5 on risk assessment). An example might be checking the criminal record of all volunteers working with vulnerable clients and taking relevant action, such as refusing to allow a person to become a volunteer if they do not agree to be vetted under the Children's Act 1989.

In order to protect your organisation, you are advised to follow good practice, and ensure that:

♦ members of your governing body and everyone involved in the organisation's activities understand the relevant parts of the law and their duty of care to everyone who uses the organisation's premises, makes use of its products and services or takes part in its activities;

♦ employees, volunteers and others who carry out the organisation's activities are properly recruited, inducted, trained and supervised;

♦ you have clearly defined the nature and limits of tasks that employees and volunteers carry out, making it clear when authority must be obtained;

♦ suitable records are kept of all incidents involving personal injury, loss or damage (and any near misses or threats);

♦ your organisation has a clear procedure for dealing with complaints relating to health and safety.

When is a volunteer not a volunteer?

Recent industrial tribunals have considered people who were apparently volunteers to be employees in the eyes of the law. Organisations should be cautious about assuming that people have the status of volunteer – in one recent case, a person worked four mornings a week and was paid £40 per week for expenses, although she lived nearby, did not take lunch breaks and may not have incurred any expenses at all. The tribunal referred to these facts in deciding that the volunteer was in fact an employee as far as the law is concerned.

It is difficult to obtain a watertight definition of a volunteer, but for the purposes of this book a volunteer is understood to be someone who voluntarily gives their time or professional expertise for the benefit of a third party and is not, nor expects to be, rewarded in any way, other than having bona fide expenses reimbursed.

In the introduction, we strongly recommended that all organisations, including those without any employees, follow the requirements of health and safety legislation as outlined in this book. If you adopt the same standard of care that is owed to employees towards your volunteers and members, then you can be confident that in the eyes of the law you will be seen to be carrying out your health and safety duty of care in a responsible manner.

Examples of where a duty of care may arise

A duty of care can arise in many ways which may not always be apparent, for example through:

- *loaning equipment to others;*
- *cleaning cars;*
- *undertaking charity walks;*
- *running fetes or fairs;*
- *sporting activities (such as swimming);*
- *events involving animals;*
- *having visitors and contractors on your premises;*
- *occupying premises;*
- *controlling a group on premises not in your ownership;*
- *adopting differing standards of duties towards children compared with adults.*

The list is almost endless and serves as a reminder that vigilance is of the utmost importance.

Chapter 2
Your health and safety policy – statement of intent

A health and safety policy is the foundation stone for developing health and safety practices within any organisation. The policy declares the degree of commitment that those who manage the organisation have towards the health and safety of everyone who will be involved in the organisation's activities – members of the governing body, employees, volunteers, members, users and the general public. It describes the strategies and procedures by which health and safety in the organisation will be managed, and it names those people responsible for carrying them out.

Your safety policy should be a working document which should be used in the induction and training of both staff and volunteers. It should be revised regularly to ensure that procedures are still relevant to the organisation's activities, and that they are being carried out as intended.

By law,[1] employers who have five or more employees must:

♦ have a written health and safety policy;
♦ communicate it to employees and anyone else working under your organisation's control (including volunteers and contractors);
♦ make it available for inspection;
♦ review it regularly.

If you have fewer than five employees, we strongly recommend that you have a health and safety policy in writing (even though this is not compulsory), as it will help to clarify procedures and areas of responsibility, and it should help to make people in your organisation more aware of health and safety issues.

A health and safety policy document

A health and safety policy document is in three parts:

Part 1 – The general statement of policy
This is the statement of your organisation's commitment in writing to tackle health and safety issues. It must be dated and signed.

Part 2 – Responsibility for carrying out the statement of intent
Those persons with specific areas of responsibility – such as those in charge of fire procedures or first aid provision – should be identified.

Part 3 – The arrangements and procedures
The systems and arrangements you have made to comply with your statement of intent will form this part of the policy – for instance, your fire procedures, accident reporting, copies of risk assessments and any other specific procedures you have set up.

The general statement of policy is a demonstration of your commitment to improving health and safety procedures. Drawing it up is something you can do straight away.

A basic health and safety policy is printed in appendix 2 at the end of this book – you can fill in part 1 now. You will start to prepare the documents to create the rest of the policy as you work through the book. Remember, it is not just a case of filling in the blank spaces – you will

---

1 *The Health and Safety at Work etc. Act 1974.*

need to have a clear strategy for establishing health, safety and welfare within your organisation.

When you have completed this chapter, turn to the checklist on page 65 and tick off the actions you have taken.

 Volunteers only

Organisations with volunteers only are not obliged to produce a health and safety policy, but they still have a duty of care to volunteers. A policy will help you and your organisation to clarify procedures and areas of responsibility.

We strongly recommend you to carry out the same procedures as above to produce a policy, communicating it to volunteers and reviewing it regularly.

Chapter 3
Registering your activity

Every organisation which has paid employees must register the existence of their premises and activities, regardless of size or location. Health and safety legislation is enforced by either the Health and Safety Executive (HSE) or the Environmental Health Service Department (EHSD), which is part of the local council. The local fire brigade also requires notification of your existence because it has responsibility for fire precautions (see chapter 8).

The enforcement agency with which you register is determined by the type of work your organisation is involved in. Generally speaking, work that involves high risks (such as construction or manufacture), is under the authority of the HSE, while lower-risk activities (like retailing) are looked after by the local EHSD. If you are starting up a new organisation with paid staff, you should give the appropriate agency as much notice as possible before you open or begin operating. It is never too late to register, but failure to register your activity can result in a fine.

All types of activity are required to register. Even if you are only employing people to work on a temporary summer playscheme, the location and activity will still need to be registered.

Who should you register with?

1 For an activity involving manufacture or repair (such as clothing manufacture, furniture repair, craft making, printing or processing activities), you need to inform your local HSE. To do this, obtain Form F9 from your local HSE office (listed in appendix 3), and complete and return it. For building construction use Form F10, which can also be obtained from your local HSE office and should also be returned there.

2 For an activity involving retailing or storage, such as catering (see chapter 13, *Food hygiene*), warehousing, office work or leisure activities (see below), you should inform your local EHSD by completing form OSR1. EHSDs are listed in your local telephone directory under the local council.

If you are unsure which category your activity falls into, ring the HSE Infoline on 08701 545500 (open 8.30a.m. to 5p.m., Monday to Friday), or try the HSE website (www.hsedirect.com).

Activities for which you may need a licence

For some activities, you will require a licence from the appropriate enforcement agency. In the voluntary sector, some of the most relevant licences are for entertainment and food. If you have any doubts or queries about needing a licence, contact your local EHSD or the HSE. For instance, if you are running an event where music and dancing are the main attractions you will require an entertainments licence.

♦ If the venue is already licensed, then you must comply with the conditions of the licence, such as the maximum numbers allowed to attend the event. You must also comply with the current fire precaution arrangements in force at the venue.

♦ For a venue which is not licensed (such as a building not normally used for entertainments), you must apply for a temporary entertainments licence from your Local Authority Licensing Section.

The main items of concern regarding health and safety in respect of granting an entertainments licence are:
* the potential fire hazards;
* the requirements for fire exits;
* fire escape procedures;
* fire-fighting equipment (see chapter 8);
* the safety of electrical equipment.

For example, you decide to hold a barn dance as a fundraising event, and a local farmer has agreed you can use his old barn. Your organisation would have to address all the points above to ensure the event is held safely.

Other activities for which a licence is required include the following:
* an event which involves the sale of alcohol;
* running an outdoor activity centre;
* the provision of food.

 Volunteers only

Organisations with volunteers only do not normally need to register their activity unless they are involved in some dangerous process or event, such as putting on a fireworks display. Check with your local EHSD if you have any queries.

However, the following are exceptions:
* If your organisation owns or controls premises, you will need to obtain a fire certificate (see chapter 8).
* You need to register premises with the EHSD if food is prepared, stored, supplied or sold there on five or more days in any five-week period. The five days do not have to be consecutive. The registration requirements also apply to the provision of food out of doors (see chapter 13).

When you have completed this chapter, turn to the checklist on page 65 and tick off the actions you have taken.

Chapter 4
Insurance

Every voluntary organisation, whatever its size or activities, should examine its insurance cover at least once a year. All too frequently, it is only when an accident or other unforeseen event occurs that insurance is discussed, often because the organisation finds that it is not insured for the incident and is facing costs for liability.

Responsibility

It is up to the members of the governing body of your organisation to make sure you have the appropriate insurance cover. Remember, legal responsibility can be shared between all of the members of the governing body, as illustrated in the case of the Scout Council below. We recommend that a senior member of your organisation takes responsibility for all insurance matters, preparing an annual insurance report for presentation to the management committee at least once a year.

In a tragic case, a child from a school visiting a Scouts' activity centre drowned in the centre's pool, which resulted in the local Scout Council being fined £10,000 with £7,000 costs for failing to ensure the safety of visitors. The judgement was made against the entire Scout Council, not individual members of the Council.

Insurance cover should be additional to, rather than instead of, action taken to reduce risks. In the example above, the local authority which brought the case against the Scout Council issued a statement to organisations warning them to consider the health and safety of visitors to their sites, as well as that of their own members and employees. It added: 'it is not sufficient to assume visiting organisations will act safely ... insurance cover is no substitute for the proper control of risks'.

Finding appropriate insurance

Insurance needs for charitable organisations can be very complex. It is good advice to explain your needs to an insurance broker. There are a number of insurance companies and brokers that specialise in insuring the voluntary sector – you could ask a colleague or the local Council for Voluntary Services for a recommendation.

Although insurance policies may be obtained more cheaply by approaching insurance companies directly, a good insurance broker can take you through the endless types of insurance and costs, advising you on which risks your organisation should be insured against and on which policy is best for you. They will also remind you to renew your insurance policy and help you to make any claims against it.

Don't forget: if the activities of your organisation change, you should consult your insurance company or broker as you may need additional insurance cover.

Types of insurance

1 Employers' liability insurance

Employers' liability insurance covers your paid employees in the event of an accident, disease or injury caused or made worse as a result of work. All employers are required by law to ensure that any liability to a paid employee is covered by such insurance.

By law,[1] employers must:
♦ take out and maintain an approved insurance policy with an authorised insurer to cover paid employees, including temporary

1 Employers' Liability (Compulsory Insurance) Regulations 1998. NB: The law does not apply to people working in Great Britain for less than 14 consecutive days, to close relatives of the employer, or to independent contractors engaged by the employer. Nor does it apply to persons working abroad.

workers, part time workers, casual workers and apprentices;

♦ seek advice as to the extent of the insurance cover required for their activities;

♦ prominently display the certificate of insurance in the workplace where it can be seen by employees.

It may be necessary to treat trainees as employees for insurance purposes (especially those on government training schemes and people serving community orders). If in any doubt, talk to your insurers or project sponsors.

You should also check the insurance status of any secondees or people on work placements with your organisation.

What is not covered by employers' liability insurance

♦ Employers' liability insurance covers only illness, injury or death caused by the employer's negligence (see chapter 1). The insurance does not normally cover situations where the employer has not been found to have been negligent.

 Volunteers only

In some recent legal cases, voluntary workers have been considered by industrial tribunals to be employees, and therefore entitled to the same terms and conditions as paid employees, including employers' liability insurance cover. 'Employees' are any individuals working full or part time, doing manual, clerical or any other kind of work, who have a contract of employment with the employer. This applies whether the contract is written, or agreed verbally. Don't forget that paying a fixed rate for expenses rather than reimbursing actual expenses may mean that a volunteer becomes an employee in law.

If there is any doubt about the legal status of your voluntary workers, you are well advised to obtain specialist advice on the matter, and you should consider seeking advice about the need for employers' liability insurance for volunteers.

♦ The insurance should cover any legal costs resulting from your actions or negligence, but it will not pay for fines.

♦ The insurance does not cover personal property or the organisation's property or equipment.

2 Public liability insurance

Although there is no strict legal obligation to have public liability insurance, any organisation which owns premises or arranges public events is strongly recommended to take out such insurance. Members of the governing body may be in breach of trust if they have control of or own premises and do not take out public liability insurance, as that would mean they have not discharged their duty in protecting the assets of the organisation.

This insurance covers individuals (other than employees) and organisations in the event of an accident, injury or death, or damage to, or loss of property caused through the negligence of someone acting with the organisation's authority, including the actions of your volunteers.

If volunteers, trainees and members of the governing body are not identified in the employers' liability insurance, they should be explicitly included in the public liability insurance – check with your insurance company.

It is a good idea to display your public liability certificate where your members can see it. You should make every organisation member aware of what the insurance policy covers and – more important – what it does not cover.

What is not covered by public liability insurance

♦ There are some common exclusions in public liability insurance, for example certain high-risk activities such as aviation activities, hot air ballooning, parachute or bungee jumping. Remember: if your organisation becomes involved in any *new* and potentially high-risk activities, they may be excluded from your public liability insurance policy – check with your insurers.

- Public liability insurance does not normally cover special events – see section 5b.
- The insurance does not cover personal property or the organisation's property or equipment.

3 Personal accident insurance

Organisations may wish to take out personal accident insurance to cover accidents or deaths arising from paid work or volunteering, but not due to the organisation's negligence. In other words, it would not matter whose fault it was if a person were injured or killed while working for the organisation – a sum of money would still be paid to the person injured and/or to support their dependants.

If the benefit is extended to members of the governing body, the Charity Commission's permission must be sought first.

4 Product liability insurance

This type of insurance covers organisations who make, manufacture, sell or supply goods if there are claims made against them arising from death, illness or injury caused by products sold or supplied. You may require this insurance if your organisation undertakes activities such as supplying reconditioned computers to other groups, or selling items of furniture.

5 Other areas

Other areas which need considering include:

a) Contractors

Contractors and self-employed personnel hired for any work with your organisation should have their own public liability insurance. This will cover your members and property against any injury or damages caused by them. You should check that they have this insurance.

b) Special events

If your organisation is organising a special event that is not normally part of your ordinary activities – for instance, a fireworks display or an outing for children – you should first check if your existing insurance covers this type of event or activity. If not, think very seriously about taking out additional insurance to cover the event or activity.

c) Other persons/organisations attending your event

You are advised to ensure that all other organisations attending or supplying a service at any event you organise – such as a catering unit at a village festival – have their own valid public liability insurance policy. This will help to indemnify you in the event of something going wrong as a result of their activity, for example food poisoning.

d) Road vehicles
(i) Organisation's vehicles

By law, if your organisation operates its own vehicles, you must ensure that they are properly insured and only used for the purposes stated in the insurance documents.

You should read your insurance documents carefully and be aware of any exclusion clauses. Some exclusions are very common – for example, drivers under 25 years of age are often excluded from driving minibuses unless named on the policy; while people with certain medical conditions such as epilepsy or heart disease may be excluded from cover on your insurance.

Remember, it is extremely important to keep your insurance company up-to-date if drivers' medical conditions change. Driving convictions must also be notified to your insurer. Not telling your insurance company about any changes could invalidate your drivers' insurance.

(ii) Own vehicles

If your organisation allows or expects paid employees or volunteers to use their own motor vehicles for work purposes (called business use)

– such as delivering goods, driving to work-related meetings or picking up pensioners to visit a lunch club – you should make sure that their motor insurance covers them for the activity.

Personnel should immediately stop using their vehicles for voluntary work until they have consulted with their own insurance company and established their insurance position, or until other additional insurance cover is arranged.

A simple standard letter for drivers to send to their insurance company can easily be drawn up. You could also produce a declaration for the driver to sign, confirming that they have obtained approval from their insurance company to use their vehicle for business purposes. And yearly checks should be made to ensure that insurance cover has been renewed.

(iii) Occasional use insurance

Your organisation can arrange insurance cover for paid staff and volunteers to use their private cars for the organisation's business on an occasional basis.

(iv) No claims bonus

Your organisation may wish to consider taking out insurance to protect the no claims bonus of its drivers while they are carrying out duties on behalf of the organisation. If you are a charitable organisation, then you should obtain the Charity Commission's consent first.

(v) Large organisations

If your organisation has a lot of drivers, it may be prudent to take out motor contingency insurance, which provides third party cover to employees and/or volunteers if their own insurance has lapsed or been invalidated. However, remember that third party insurance provides only limited cover.

You should contact your insurance company for more details. Advice may also be available from your local authority, or the DVLC (Driver and Vehicle Licensing Centre), regarding specific licences required (for minibuses, for example).

When you have completed this chapter, turn to the checklist on page 65 and tick off the actions you have taken.

Chapter 5
Risk assessment

Risk assessment is a requirement of the Management of Health and Safety at Work Regulations 1999. If you have more than five employees, the risk assessments have to be written down. We strongly recommend that these should be included in the Arrangements section of your health and safety policy (see page 71). If you employ fewer than five people, you are still obliged to carry out assessments, but you do not have to record them in writing. However, we strongly recommend that you do so anyway, as they define responsibilities and they may help to make people in your organisation more aware of health and safety.

♦ A hazard is anything that has the potential to cause harm (such as a slippery floor).

♦ Risk is the likelihood of a hazard causing harm.

Risk assessment involves:

♦ identifying the hazards resulting from the organisation's activities which could affect anyone, including members of the governing body, employees, volunteers and the general public;

♦ assessing the risk of the hazards occurring;

♦ evaluating the likely severity of the outcome;

♦ eliminating the hazards if possible, or else reducing them to the lowest level of risk that is reasonably practicable.

Carrying out a risk assessment

Assessing risk requires detailed knowledge of the working practices normally only found among people who are experienced in doing the work. We believe that assessing risk cannot be done properly without the cooperation and involvement of your employees and volunteers. Remember that you also have a duty to consult with safety representatives (see chapter 15); they have often received excellent health and safety training and will be able to assist you in carrying out joint risk assessments. You may need to request specialist help as well (the HSE and your Environmental Health Services Department can offer advice – contact the HSE Infoline on 08701 545500 or the HSE website, www.hsedirect.com, or your local EHSD – details will be in your local phone book).

A number of methods are used to carry out a risk assessment. One of these methods is shown below.

Step 1	Look for the hazard.
Step 2	Decide who might be harmed, and how.
Step 3	Evaluate the risks arising from the hazard and decide whether existing control measures are adequate or if more should be done.
Step 4	Record your findings and insert these into your health and safety management document. Inform all staff and volunteers.
Step 5	Review your assessment from time to time and make changes if necessary.

The results of the risk assessment will be useful in determining gaps in skills or knowledge in your organisation, which will help to identify training needs.

When doing the assessment, you should walk around your premises with an employee or volunteer, or safety representative if available, and take a critical look at your surroundings to see what could potentially cause harm or injury to any staff members, volunteers or members of the public. Don't forget to ask other people's opinion during this process – they may mention problems that you are not aware of, and involving them in the process usually means that they will be more committed to the outcome.

This helps to ensure that any action you take deals adequately with the hazard. It is also important to ensure that everyone is aware of any changes made. This process will help to monitor the effectiveness of the risk assessment and the action taken.

A risk assessment should be carried out for each of your activities or events. And you should repeat the exercise regularly to account for any changes or new practices.

▼ Volunteers only

Organisations with volunteers only are not strictly required by law to carry out risk assessments, but they are strongly advised to adopt the same risk assessment methods explained in this section. You should be aware that you have a legal responsibility of duty of care (see chapter 1).

A risk assessment will outline where action is needed, and where priorities lie, so that an organisation can decide where to concentrate time and resources when beginning to develop its health and safety procedures.

Organisations with both employees and voluntary workers are morally, if not legally obliged to provide the same standards of protection to volunteers as those enjoyed by employees.

The findings of your risk assessments and the action required to either eliminate or reduce the problem should be included in the Arrangements section of your health and safety policy – see page 71.

Example: A group of volunteers and paid helpers have arranged to take special needs children on an outing to a local shopping centre. The group listed the following points to be considered as part of their risk assessment:

- *Potential risks to both children and helpers need to be considered.*
- *Any concerns from parents and guardians should be addressed.*
- *The ratio of carers to children has to be worked out, depending on the needs of each child.*
- *There must be suitable wheelchair access in the centre.*
- *Lifts or escalators need to be identified so the carers do not have to carry any of the children.*
- *Parking spaces should be close to the centre, to prevent a long walk which may increase the likelihood of children getting lost or becoming agitated.*
- *Potential problems should be thought through – for example, agreeing a central meeting point in the shopping area in case any members of the group become separated from the rest.*
- *Other organisations who have arranged similar trips could be contacted and consulted.*
- *All carers should be briefed on the day of the trip, and given the mobile telephone number of the trip supervisor in case of problems.*

Note: there are no hard and fast rules in carrying out a risk assessment – you need to consider the particular circumstances relevant to your organisation's activity.

When you have completed this chapter, turn to the checklist on page 65 and tick off the actions you have taken.

RISK ASSESSMENT FORM Part 1

Location/Activity: Walk organised by the Fresh Air Club for 12th May 2001

Assessor: Brenda Boots

Assessment date: 23/4/01
Review date: 12/5/01

Accepted by Senior Manager (signature):
Andy Pack

Item no.	Hazards/activity	Risks	Current control measures	All personnel involved/affected	Present risk rating high/medium/low	Is further action required? Yes/No
1	Organised walk for adults	People becoming separated from main party		All participants	Medium, depending on size of group and weather conditions	Yes
2		People being injured	Some members of club already have first aid qualifications	All participants	Low	No
3		Some participants not fit enough to complete the walk		Newcomers to the club	Medium	Yes

RISK ASSESSMENT FORM   Part 2

Item no.	Further action		Assumed risk rating following further action e.g. CoSHH, DSE	Are further assessments required? List assessments
	Short-term action	**Long-term action**		
1	• Limit numbers of people on walk • Insist that leader of walk and deputy have adequate training and experience • Ensure that participants have suitable clothing and equipment (including food, whistle, survival bag and mobile phone) in case they are separated from main group • Check that all participants are covered by the insurance of group • Plan alternative walk for poor weather conditions, and check local weather forecast on day of walk	• Encourage members of group to undertake training in map-reading and orienteering • Obtain survival supplies for loan to new members of group	Low	Reassessment on day of activity
3	• Carry out assessments on fitness levels of new members (e.g. by involving them in shorter and local walks) • Leaders should check participants during walk • Select walk which has half-way stop where people can retire from walk if required	• Induction training for new members	Low	No

RISK ASSESSMENT FORM Part 1

Location/Activity: Stacking books in charity shop

Assessor: Billy Books

Assessment date: 1/5/01

Review date: 1/8/01

Accepted by Senior Manager (signature):

B. Mark

Item no.	Hazards/activity	Risks	Current control measures	All personnel involved/affected	Present risk rating high/medium/low	Is further action required? Yes/No
1	Storage of books on high shelves	Injuries caused by falling books, due to overloading of shelves	None	Staff, volunteers and customers	High	Yes
	Storage of books on high shelves	Injuries due to manual handling of loads, i.e. carrying, lifting, stretching	Step-ladder used by staff to assist in stacking shelves	Staff and volunteers	High	Yes

RISK ASSESSMENT FORM Part 2

Item no.	Further action		Assumed risk rating following further action e.g. CoSHH, DSE	Are further assessments required? List assessments
	Short-term action	Long-term action		
1	• Heavier books to be stored on lower shelves only • Ensure that shelves are attached to wall of shop • Ensure that shelves are strong enough for the weight of books – if not, strengthen or replace shelves • Supervisor to check storage of books on high shelves	N/A	Low	Manual handling
2	• Restricted use of step-ladders to people who have been trained in safe lifting techniques	N/A	Medium	Manual handling

Chapter 6
Health, safety and welfare

Health, safety and welfare legislation has been introduced to improve the working environment, to ensure that the risks to health are reduced to the lowest possible level and that a suitable and safe place for work is provided. By law,[1] employers must provide:

+ a safe place of work – i.e. one that is clean, tidy and free from risk;
+ safe systems of work – e.g. adequate guarding of machines or proper use of chemicals;
+ adequate supervision – employees should not be left to their own devices, but should be checked to ensure that they are working safely;
+ training and information – employees must have sufficient skills and knowledge to carry out their work safely;
+ a written safety policy (if they employ five or more persons) – see chapter 2.

Legislation also places a duty on employees to:

+ look after themselves and others – they must not act in an unsafe manner or put themselves or others in danger;
+ cooperate with the employer in matters of health and safety – they should carry out health and safety instructions.

A list of regulations, including those which apply to special risks, is provided in appendix 4 (other

legislation may be relevant to your organisation, depending on your situation).

1 The Management of Health and Safety at Work Regulations 1999

These require that health and safety legislation is implemented at all places of work. Employers have a duty to identify the potential risks to employees and others, and assess when they could occur and who could be affected. If risks are identified, employers should take appropriate action to eliminate or minimise them.

You may have to obtain information from the HSE, outside suppliers of products that you use, and other sources.

By law employers must:

+ identify and assess all risks of hazards associated with their activity which may have an effect on the health and safety of their employees and others;
+ carry out risk assessments using persons who are competent (see chapter 5);
+ take action to eliminate or reduce hazards;
+ record the arrangements made (if five or more persons are employed);
+ review arrangements as and when changes occur;
+ cooperate with other employers if their employees share the same risk;
+ provide health and safety training for employees and temporary workers.

You are advised to begin the assessments in-house, but if you have any difficulties at all, don't

 Volunteers only

Organisations with volunteers only are not bound by these regulations, but they do need to ensure that their working conditions are safe. It would be hard to justify having lower standards of health and safety for volunteers compared with paid staff, simply because the law does not demand it (see chapter 1).

---

1 *Health and Safety at Work etc. Act 1974.*

hesitate to ask for information or advice from outside organisations such as outside suppliers, or contact the HSE Infoline on 08701 545500.

Employees also have a part to play, as they are obliged to:
♦ work to procedures specified;
♦ cooperate with training and instructions given by the employer;
♦ inform the employer of hazards at the workplace.

In this way, everyone in the workplace has a role in ensuring that the conditions meet the legal requirements.

2 The Workplace (Health, Safety and Welfare) Regulations 1992

These regulations are aimed at protecting employees' health from injury or long-term illness; ensuring their safety by affording protection from immediate danger and their welfare by providing facilities for personal comfort at work.

The health aspects are covered by ensuring:
♦ adequate ventilation – e.g. for workplace fumes and for bathrooms (toilets should be ventilated to the outside);
♦ a reasonable temperature, at least 16° C (there is no maximum)
♦ suitable lighting;
♦ clean floors, walls, furniture, ceilings, windows and fittings;
♦ adequate seating if work can be undertaken while sitting down;
♦ no undue reaching, bending or stretching is required when using equipment or machinery;
♦ enough space for each person (the minimum should be 3.7 square metres (40 square feet)

of floor space; 11 cubic metres (400 cubic feet) of air space).

Safety is promoted by providing:
♦ safe premises, floors and stairs – floors should be clean and tidy, with no tripping hazards;
♦ suitably maintained equipment or machinery;
♦ space for people's safe movement – they must be able to enter and leave safely;
♦ the fencing-off of openings from which people are likely to fall;
♦ safe storage for all materials and goods;
♦ safety glass in windows where appropriate;
♦ control of vehicles where pedestrians are at risk – such as traffic calming measures.

The welfare aspects are covered by providing:
♦ a sufficient number of toilets for the number of people on the premises – consult your local EHSD on this;
♦ suitable washing facilities with hot and cold water, soap and towels;
♦ facilities if required for changing, drying and storing clothes;
♦ accessible drinking water;
♦ suitable facilities for rest and eating;
♦ suitable provision for non-smokers.

3 The Provision and Use of Work Equipment Regulations 1998

All equipment provided by the employer for use at work should comply with these regulations. The main provisions are to ensure that all work equipment is suitable for its purpose and used only for that purpose, that it is maintained adequately, and that it is restricted to the individuals given the task of using it.

Again, the key aspects are that the risks of using equipment should be assessed and that measures should be taken to protect against potential hazards arising from using the equipment. Ideally this would involve eliminating the hazard, but, as a last resort, protective equipment may be issued. Training should be provided for people using and maintaining the equipment.

4 The Manual Handling Operations Regulations 1992

These require a risk assessment (see chapter 5) to be carried out in all cases where employees have to carry, lift, push or pull items as part of their employment.

Employers should avoid any manual handling operations which involve the risk of injury. The assessment should identify any unnecessary operations.

If an operation cannot be avoided, then employers need to take steps to reduce the risk of injury, give information about the object to be moved (such as its weight, its heaviest side) and provide a safe system of work. The assessment must be reviewed periodically or when changes are made.

There is also an obligation on employees to make full use of the guidelines provided as a result of the assessment.

Key considerations

As part of your manual handling risk assessment, you may wish to consider the following issues:

(a) Decide whether it is possible to avoid handling the load. For example, can it be done mechanically or can a truck be used?

(b) Check whether the following are needed to carry out the job:
♦ special information/training;
♦ special capabilities (e.g. training or experience);
♦ personal protective equipment – see section 5 (note that personal protective clothing must allow for free movement during manual handling).

(c) Ensure specific instructions are given to persons not to lift loads if they consider the load is:
♦ too heavy;
♦ too bulky/unwieldy;
♦ too difficult to get hold of;
♦ of a dangerous nature (e.g. hot, sharp, a hazardous chemical).

(d) Those in charge should ensure that people are given advice and assistance before starting the job. Consider individual circumstances – for instance, in the case of people with health problems or women who are pregnant.

(e) Assess whether the job involves any of the following movements (which increase the chance of injury) when carrying or lifting:
♦ the load being held away from the upper body;
♦ twisting;
♦ bending;
♦ reaching upwards;
♦ carrying the load on one side of the body;
♦ carrying the load for a long distance;
♦ too much pushing or pulling;
♦ repetitive handling;
♦ movements where the rate of work is governed by factors outside the operator's control (e.g. unloading a conveyor).

(f) There must be rest and/or recovery periods.

(g) The area where the job is to be done should be free from risk and there must be:
♦ ample space to allow people to work and to get to the load;
♦ an even and level floor with no tripping or slipping hazards;
♦ reasonable temperature/humidity and air movement;
♦ a good level of lighting.

5 The Personal Protective Equipment at Work Regulations 1992

A risk assessment should be carried out first of all. The regulations require that adequate protective equipment and clothing must be made available where appropriate, in cases where risks to safety and health cannot be controlled by other means. The regulations apply only to clothes and equipment used for health and safety reasons (uniforms and items that do not have a protective function are not included under these regulations). Note that it is not sufficient to merely provide protective equipment without also assessing the hazards in order to eliminate or reduce them.

Any personal protective equipment provided should be in good condition, replaced when found defective and stored in a suitable place when not in use. The user should also be provided with information about the equipment, and instruction and training in its use.

The employer must take reasonable steps to ensure that the equipment is used. Employees are obliged to use it and to report any loss or defect.

6 The Health and Safety (Display Screen Equipment) Regulations 1992

Special provisions apply to the use of visual display units (VDUs) and for those employees who use VDUs as a significant part of their work. They generally apply only to desktop computer-type monitors, although laptops are included if they are in prolonged use.

Employers must:
♦ provide suitable and sufficient assessment of the work station and review it if there is any change;

♦ reduce risks identified by the risk assessment (see chapter 5);
♦ ensure that the work is interrupted by breaks and changes to reduce the workload;
♦ provide appropriate eyesight tests, to be completed by a competent person at regular intervals (every two years is generally considered to be reasonable);
♦ supply corrective glasses if required;
♦ provide training and information to ensure that people are not exposed to unnecessary risks.

The assessment should cover such risks as upper limb disorder (also known as repetitive strain disorder, or RSI). HSE guidance acknowledges that there are difficulties in predicting the likelihood of musculo-skeletal problems, but suggests that users are encouraged to report any relevant symptoms at an early stage.

The regulations do not acknowledge that there is a link between using VDUs and pregnancy problems; however, the possibility of a risk has not been ruled out. The regulations suggest only that you discuss the issue with pregnant women in order to reduce stress or anxiety, but in our opinion it would be good practice to provide alternative work if possible.

Key considerations

As part of your VDU risk assessment, you may wish to consider the following issues:

The use of visual display equipment should not be a source of risk to users. The following conditions must be achievable on computer systems in order to prevent risks to health.

The equipment
(a) Display screen
♦ The screen image should be stable with no flickering.
♦ The brightness/contrast control should be easily adjusted.
♦ The screen must tilt and swivel easily.
♦ The screen height must be adjustable.
♦ The screen must be free from glare.

♦ The screen should be regularly cleaned.
♦ The size of the screen should meet current legal requirements.

(b) Keyboard

♦ The keyboard should be adjustable to allow a comfortable working position.
♦ There must be sufficient space in front of the keyboard to support the user's hands.

(c) Work desk

♦ The work desk should be large enough to allow flexibility in the positioning of all the equipment.
♦ The surface must not cause reflective glare.
♦ A document holder should be available if needed.

(d) Work chair

♦ The chair must be stable.
♦ It must allow the operator freedom of movement.
♦ The height of the chair must be adjustable.
♦ The back must be adjustable for both height and tilt.
♦ A foot-rest must be provided if required.

The work environment
(a) Space requirements

♦ Sufficient space must be provided around the work station.

(b) Lighting

♦ The lighting has to be satisfactory and suitable for the vision requirements of the user.
♦ Disturbing glare and reflection on the display screen from light fittings, windows and walls must be avoided.

(c) Power

♦ Cables must not provide tripping hazards.
♦ Sufficient electrical sockets should be available to prevent overloading and unnecessary trailing cables.

(d) Noise

♦ The equipment noise should be low and not distract attention or disturb normal speech.

Heat emission and radiation

♦ The heat emitted from the equipment must be dissipated equally in the work environment and not cause concentrated hot-spots.

The software

♦ The software should be easy to understand.
♦ If possible, the software should allow the pace of work to be varied.

The users

♦ Training is required on:
  – use of the work station;
  – health and safety aspects of the work station;
  – ergonomics.
♦ Users need to:
  – understand eye and eyesight testing;
  – be aware of changes in eye discomfort, especially if contact lenses are worn, and seek advice as soon as any change is noticed;
  – understand that regular work breaks must be taken when there are lengthy periods at the VDU.

The details covered above are not comprehensive, but they do give you a good idea of the areas which have to be considered. You need to assess your own premises and work activities, preferably with input from all those who use the equipment and from outside advisers where necessary (you can contact the HSE Infoline on 08701 545500).

When you have completed this chapter, turn to the checklist on page 65 and tick off the actions you have taken.

Chapter 7
CoSHH assessment

All workplaces with employees must carry out an assessment under the Control of Substances Hazardous to Health (CoSHH) Regulations 1994, which require every employer to assess the workplace for risks to health from substances used there. They must take all necessary steps to control any risk identified. If an assessment has not already been done, it should be carried out immediately to comply with the regulations.

What is a hazardous substance?

A hazardous substance can be a liquid, solid, dust, powder or gas which can damage health when it comes into contact with skin or eyes; or enters the body through the skin; or is breathed in, swallowed or even transferred to the mouth via contaminated hands.

Many substances used or generated at work are hazardous to health. Working procedures should aim to minimise the effects of these substances on the health of all employees. You need to consider the possible ill effects of all substances in use – assessment is the key.

You must then prevent your employees from being exposed to hazardous substances, using less harmful substitutes or different methods of work to reduce the risk where possible.

Any substance can be potentially dangerous in certain circumstances. For instance, some common household bleaches, when mixed with certain other household cleaners, can give off a poisonous gas which is extremely dangerous in confined spaces. Other substances such as pesticides, wood dusts and solvent paints may not cause immediate harm but may lead to serious disease in later life. Suppliers of

Hazard data sheets
If you use any hazardous substances, you should obtain hazard data sheets from the manufacturer or supplier of each substance. This information can then be used to help you complete the CoSHH assessment.

CoSHH assessment
This identifies how each substance is used within your organisation and who is responsible for its use, ordering, storage, etc.

substances must supply hazard data sheets where requested, which will list safety precautions to be taken when using their products.

The hazard data sheet and the label on the product container or wrapping should show one of the following signs to indicate the main hazards:

 Toxic
 Corrosive
 Highly flammable
 Explosive
 Harmful
 Oxidising

Carrying out the assessment

In many organisations the chemicals used may not be very hazardous, so a CoSHH assessment would be quite straightforward. For example, if your organisation only uses mild cleaning agents, then you would need to ensure that anyone likely to use them is made fully aware of any potential hazards, and how to store the substances, how to deal with spillages, etc.

If more hazardous substances are used, then a more detailed assessment should be carried out by a person who understands the requirements of the CoSHH regulations and approved codes of practice. They also need the ability to get all the necessary information, as well as the knowledge and skill to make correct decisions regarding the risks and precautions needed.

The HSE's step-by-step guidance booklet, 'CoSHH Assessments', recommends that, if possible, the assessment process should be started in-house, using the expertise of people doing the work. Remember that you have a duty to consult with safety representatives (see chapter 15) – they have often received excellent health and safety training and will be able to assist you in carrying out a risk assessment. Depending on the type and nature of the work you undertake, an outside specialist may be required to help you make your assessment (the HSE can offer advice).

A CoSHH assessment should follow the same steps as used above for a risk assessment (see chapter 5) to determine the precautions required to protect the health of employees and others exposed to substances. The CoSHH regulations set out essential measures that the employer and employees have to take, and in order to comply you have to take the following steps.

Step 1 – Look for the hazard

Identify the hazardous substances present. Consider the risks they present to people's health if the risk is significant.

Step 2 – Decide who might be harmed, and how

Anyone who uses the substance could be at risk, while others could be affected indirectly (for

instance, by working near to where the substance is being used). You must also consider others who could be exposed without being aware of the hazards, including children or animals. Your method of working will need to include a control method to reduce any risk to children or any others who may be affected by the task.

Step 3 – Evaluate the risks arising from the hazard and decide whether existing control measures are adequate or if more should be done

Exposure to a hazardous substance such as photocopier toner or solvent-based paints should be prevented if possible by providing a safer alternative. Note that if you choose a less hazardous alternative, you still have to carry out a CoSHH assessment on it.

If it is not possible to replace the substance, exposure should be limited by improving ventilation, reducing the number of people exposed or providing appropriate protective equipment.

You also have to consider ways to reduce the risks associated with using the substance you have chosen.

From the supplier's safety data sheet you will find information on:

- the hazards identified with the product;
- first aid measures;
- fire-fighting measures;
- accidental release measures;
- handling and storage;
- exposure control and personal protection;
- the physical and chemical properties of the product;
- the substance's stability and how it reacts with other products;
- toxicological information;
- the product's effects on the environment;
- how to dispose of the product;
- how to transport the product;
- regulations regarding labelling and safety phrases.

Training should be provided as required. Health surveillance will be necessary in some cases, where exposure to substances is linked to particular diseases or adverse health effects, and there is a reasonable likelihood of these occurring.

Step 4 – Record your findings and insert these into your health and safety management document. Inform all staff and volunteers

Any action taken should be recorded, and should be monitored to ensure that control measures are used and maintained. Employees should be properly informed and trained on the dangers of the substance, the risks involved and the precautions to be taken. They should also be adequately supervised, and informed of the results of any monitoring of exposure and emergency procedures.

Step 5 – Review your assessment from time to time and make changes if necessary

It is important that assessments are reassessed and reviewed. When new employees/volunteers are tackling the job for the first time, they must be given adequate training. It is also vital that any accidents or near misses are recorded and investigated, to help determine what went wrong in order that appropriate action can be taken to prevent re-occurrence (see chapter 14).

Example of an assessment
Here is an example of a CoSHH assessment of a commonly used substance – bleach. The fact that it is frequently used in domestic settings does not mean that its potential for harm should be underestimated. In this example, volunteers in a local yacht club are using bleach to clean the toilets and drains in their club house. The manufacturer's hazard data sheet has been obtained, and as a result a CoSHH assessment has been carried out.

Step 1 Look for the hazard
Members of the club conducted a safety tour of the club house, and identified bleach as a potential hazard.

Step 2 Decide who might be harmed, and how
The volunteers who carry out the cleaning and anyone using the facilities immediately after cleaning could be affected by it.

Step 3 Evaluate the risks arising from the hazards and decide whether existing control measures are adequate or more should be done
The risks were identified from the container label and hazard data sheet. A discussion was held with all volunteers involved in cleaning, to identify and standardise the control measures used.

Step 4 Record your findings and insert these into your health and safety management document. Inform all staff and volunteers
The information collated was recorded on a CoSHH assessment form (see overleaf), and placed in the health and safety policy.

Step 5 Review your assessment from time to time and make changes if necessary
It was agreed to review the procedures periodically, or if any new chemicals were introduced, or if any new volunteers were recruited.

The CoSHH assessment

The following general assessment should be used as a guide only; actual work practices must be reviewed.

Product or process (include trade names)	Thick bleach
Hazards or risks to health	Identified as an irritant. Can cause respiratory and skin problems on exposure.
Persons or groups affected	Volunteers; club-house users and visitors.
Handling precautions	To be used only by authorised personnel who have received training in the use of the substance and its potential hazards.
Route of exposure, i.e. Skin Eyes Breathing Swallowing	Absorption through the skin can lead to serious burns or reactions. There may be reactions to the eyes if taken in the air or if there are splashes. Care must be taken to avoid inhalation. All areas must be well ventilated. If bleach is swallowed the casualty should drink water to relieve burning. Vomiting must not be encouraged. In all cases medical aid must be sought immediately
Approved uses	The bleach must only be used for cleaning drains or sinks where no other substance is used.
Personal protective equipment, i.e. Goggles/visor; gloves; coveralls; respirator/mask; other (specify)	The bleach must be used in a well-ventilated area. It should be diluted one part bleach to nine parts water. The user must wear gloves, which have been made available.

The following is provided to assist in the safe handling, use and disposal of the materials described above.

Personal hygiene	Hands should be washed thoroughly after exposure.
Storage	Bleach must be stored in the domestics cupboard (key available from the manager – not to be accessed unless authorised). It should be kept out of direct sunlight and away from food at all times.
Spillage	The room should be ventilated and the area rinsed with water.
Waste disposal	Must be disposed of in the bin provided – i.e. marked 'for containers of hazardous substances' – where safety staff and volunteers will ensure safe disposal. Undiluted bleach must not enter the drain course.
For further information contact:	Refer to the manufacturer's hazard data sheet (attached) for further information. Health and safety and first aid personnel are also aware of this information and should be consulted if there are any queries.

Note: This general assessment and other information have been prepared from the manufacturer's and supplier's data. Safety in the use of any material is the responsibility of the user/s, and the information provided here should only be used as a guide.

We strongly recommend that the following leaflet is obtained from HSE: 'CoSHH: The new brief guide for employers (guidance on the main requirements of the Control of Substances Hazardous to Health (CoSHH) Regulations 1994)', HSE Books (ISBN 0 7176 1189 2).

When you have completed this chapter, turn to the *checklist on page 65* *and tick off the actions you have taken.*

 Volunteers only

Organisations with volunteers only are not strictly required by law to carry out CoSHH assessments, but they are strongly advised to adopt the same risk assessment methods explained in this section to meet their legal responsibility of duty of care (see chapter 1).

Carrying out CoSHH assessments will help you to investigate all substances used, highlight potential hazards, and outline where action is needed and where priorities lie, so that an organisation can decide where to concentrate time and resources when beginning to develop its health and safety procedures.

Organisations with both employees and voluntary workers are morally, if not legally obliged to provide the same standards of protection to volunteers as those enjoyed by employees.

Chapter 8

Fire certificate and procedures

All organisations must make arrangements to assess the risk of fire to both people and property and steps should be taken to minimise those risks. Fire can be costly to any organisation, even if no-one is injured, but may be more devastating to a voluntary organisation with limited resources.

Fire safety legislation

Legislation covering Fire Safety in the UK is about to undergo dramatic change and will affect current practice as outlined in the sections below. The Fire Precautions Act 1971 and the Fire Precautions (Workplace) Regulations 1997 have been repealed, along with many other fire safety regulations and statutes. The Draft of the Regulatory Reform (Fire Safety) Order was put before Parliament on 10th May 2004 and comes into effect during 2005. The following are the main changes:

Fire Risk Assessment is the cornerstone of the order. The risk assessment must be reviewed regularly and if necessary amended. The Risk Assessment must be formally recorded if the responsible person employs 5 or more people, the premises are licensed or the inspector requires it.

The order amends or replaces 118 pieces of legislation. The order will apply to the majority of premises and workplaces in the UK. It firmly places a responsibility on what it calls the '**Responsible Person.**'

The '**Responsible Person**' is a person who owns the premises or business or the person with control over the premises, business or activity. Where two or more responsible persons share responsibility, (tenant/landlord,

multi-tenancy building or adjacent premises) the responsible person must co-operate, share information and collaborate to carry out risk a 'Fire Risk Assessment', produce a policy, develop procedure (particularly with regards evacuation), provide staff training and carry out Fire Drills. He/she must provide and maintain clear 'Means of Escape', 'Signs', 'Notices', 'Emergency Lighting', 'Fire Detection and Alarm' and 'Extinguishers'.

'**Competent Person.**' The order also mentions a 'Competent Person'. The Responsible Person must appoint one or more Competent Persons to assist him/her.

'**Competent Person**' is someone appointed by the Responsible Person and could be anyone from the company ie, fire warden to a fire alarm service engineer, they may be directly employed or sub-contracted. The competent person must have sufficient training, knowledge, experience and ability to identify any shortfall in systems with ability to recommend action to reduce the risk identified, and is aware of their own personal limitation. Where the competent person directly employed the responsible person must ensure that he or she receives relevant training.

'**Employees.**' The responsible person must consult employees on fire safety matters and provide information for them. An employee must not act in a way that endangers him or others, must inform on co-workers who do, and co-operate with the employer. An employer cannot charge an employee for providing any fire safety measures but an employee is entitled to recover his losses if the employer fails to comply with the order.

The fire certificate

By law:[1]

◆ All premises to which members of the public have access must have either a fire certificate or an exemption certificate issued by the local fire brigade.

◆ Once a certificate has been issued, a copy should be kept on the premises.

◆ The fire brigade may decide that you qualify for exemption. This may be the case where premises are considered to be low-risk. The exemption will be given to you in writing. However, you still need to carry out a risk assessment.

Who should apply for the fire certificate?

◆ If you own or are the sole tenant or leaseholder of the premises, you as the owner or leaseholder must apply for a fire certificate.

◆ If you use premises which are not fully owned or leased to you, the owner of the premises is responsible for applying for the fire certificate and introducing those procedures specified for the premises in the certificate. However, it is the duty of each user of the premises to ensure that the fire certificate requirements are met for the areas for which they are responsible.

If you are responsible for the fire procedures, you should contact the local fire brigade to enquire about a fire certificate. The brigade will send out a fire safety officer who will advise you on your fire procedures and other needs.

When the certificate is issued it will give details of:

◆ the use of the premises;

◆ means of escape in case of fire;

◆ fire-fighting equipment required.

The certificate may also include details on any other fire precautions to be taken, as well as fire drills, training and record keeping.

In addition, the Fire Precautions (Workplace) Regulations 1997 place a duty on you to carry out a risk assessment of the fire hazards in your organisation's premises. The regulations apply to all places of work.

Fire risk assessment

The Fire Precautions (Workplace) (Amendment) Regulation 1999, introduced by the Home Office, directly require employers to take account of their general fire precautions, covering fire fighting, fire detection, emergency routes, exits and their maintenance.

The Fire Regulations also introduce a requirement:

1 for competent assistance to deal with general fire safety risks;

2 to provide employees with information on fire provisions;

3 on employers and self-employed people in a shared workplace to cooperate with others on fire provisions and to provide outside employees with comprehensive information on fire provisions.

The purpose of a fire risk assessment is to identify fire hazards and to take action to remove or reduce the likelihood of fire caused by those hazards. Important elements of the assessment include insuring that access to fire exits is kept clear, and that fire alarms and equipment are checked and serviced regularly.

A checklist of common fire hazards which could be present is as follows:

◆ flammable liquids (e.g. cleaning fluids);

◆ flammable gases (e.g. aerosols);

◆ electrical equipment producing red heat (e.g. fires, toasters, grills);

◆ damage to electrical flexes;

◆ overloading of electrical sockets;

---

1 *The Fire Precautions Act 1971.*

- storage of materials near sources of ignition;
- smoking and matches;
- emergency heating and lighting (e.g. portable gas fires, candles).

Having carried out risk assessment and taken steps to eliminate or reduce to the lowest reasonably practicable level the likelihood of the hazard causing an accident, the employer must then inform or train all staff (including employees and volunteers) in the nature of the remaining hazards, in order to enable them to be safe. An emergency plan should be introduced, and staff should be trained in it. An adequate number of competent persons should be appointed to assist in the plan – their competency will be determined by their having sufficient training, experience, knowledge and skill to perform their duties properly.

Don't forget that contractors and visitors must also be made aware of your emergency procedures.

If your activities involve hiring a hall or premises, you should ensure that the premises comply with the Fire Regulations and you should also familiarise yourself and everyone else in your organisation with the fire procedures. Depending on the type of activity concerned, you may also have responsibility for other people who are involved – for example, if you run a coffee morning in the local village hall you must ensure that everyone attending is made aware of the fire procedures (for instance, by using posters or signs).

Fire procedures in the event of fire

There is a duty on all persons in charge of

organisations to ensure that their members have knowledge of:

- the action to be taken on discovering a fire;
- what the fire alarm signal is;
- what to do when the alarm is heard;
- where their nearest fire exits are;
- the location of their fire assembly point;
- how to call the fire brigade;
- the roll-call procedure;
- special provision for people with mobility difficulties;
- restrictions on using lifts or escalators;
- conditions for re-entry to the building

In addition to this, you also need to ensure that:

- alarms (if fitted) are checked regularly;
- fire-fighting equipment is checked regularly and kept in the same, known place;
- fire exits are kept unlocked and clear while the premises are occupied;
- clear access to fire extinguishers, alarms and exits is maintained at all times;
- fire-check doors are kept closed;
- fire exit signs are in place and not covered up.

If your organisation requires people to attempt to extinguish fires, you must ensure that they are trained to use the equipment provided. You must also ensure that they are able to assess that it is safe to do so.

The regulations are enforced by the local fire brigade, which will give you advice. Contact your local brigade (telephone number in you local phone book) and enquire about your fire risks.

When you have completed this chapter, turn to the checklist on page 65 and tick off the actions you have taken.

Chapter 9
Conflict in the workplace

This chapter covers conflict involving either staff or volunteers.

Staff and volunteers in the voluntary sector often work with vulnerable individuals and people from disadvantaged sections of society, and they may be at risk of threats or violence from the very people they care for. Staff and volunteers are often expected to face their attacker(s) and even in certain cases continue to provide care for them, which can sometimes have a profound effect on those who have been attacked.

You should not underestimate the effect that verbal abuse, threats or actual violence can have on staff and volunteers. Working with such threats can have demoralising results unless people feel well equipped to deal with such situations. This should include training, and support from other members of the organisation.

By law, employers must:

♦ report all violent incidents which lead to a major injury, or to three days' absence from work, or if the person assaulted or involved in the incident is unable to do their normal work for three days as a result of the incident;[1]

♦ undertake a systematic general examination of all their work activities[2] (including the threat of violence to staff) and record the significant findings of their assessment.

In plain language, you have to consider whether the work your organisation is doing has the potential to place staff in a position where they could become victims of violent behaviour. Don't forget that violent behaviour is not just physical assault. The Health and Safety Executive has defined violence as: 'Any incident in which an employee is abused, threatened or assaulted by a member of the public in circumstances arising out of the course of his or her employment.'[3]

Volunteers, although not generally covered under the regulations mentioned in notes 1 and 2, will have some legal protection under duty of care. They do not enjoy the full protection of current health and safety law, but they should expect to have at least the same degree of protection and care that employees have.

The benefits of developing an effective policy for preventing and dealing with violence extend far beyond any statutory duty. Staff and volunteers who are properly trained, confident and well supported are better prepared to handle difficult situations and likely to be more effective in carrying out their work.

What you should do

You first need to establish whether violence or the threat of violence is a problem in your workplace. An assessment will help to clarify areas where there may be shortcomings, identify potential problem areas or simply put your mind at rest.

The general perception in your organisation may well be that you don't have a problem with violence, but remember that there may be a greater threat of violence in certain areas of work or at different times.

As an example, during the youth club session on a late Sunday afternoon a number of youth club members are displaying aggressive behaviour towards other members. Apparently they have been to the local pub with their parents to enjoy a pub lunch. The children have clearly

---

1 Since 1 April 1996, the Reporting of Injuries, Diseases and Dangerous Occurrences Regulations (RIDDOR) (see chapter 14) have included violence or the threat of violence to staff at work.
2 Management of Health and Safety at Work Regulations 1999.
3 Health and Safety Executive working definition of violence, 1988.

been drinking and turn up at the youth club and disrupt the activities of the other children. The Sunday staff are almost all volunteers and don't usually have much contact with the management, who don't work weekends.

You should undertake an assessment of how your staff and volunteers feel about the threat of violence or verbal abuse – you may wish to include the issue of bullying in your survey. This could take the form of a simple questionnaire drawn up in consultation with staff and volunteers and/or a safety representative. The issue of the survey's confidentiality should also be discussed. It is important to include all members of staff and volunteers in this exercise, particularly those whom you don't see regularly. Alternatively, your organisation may wish to discuss the matter at a meeting before you decide to take any action.

Remember that staff and volunteers need to feel confident enough to fill in the questionnaire and comfortable that any answers are not regarded as a sign of personal or professional failure. Remind everyone that the under-reporting of violence, threats or verbal abuse can potentially expose other staff members and volunteers, who may be less skilled in defusing potential violent situations, to serious risk.

You should use the results of this assessment to determine whether you need to take action to reduce the incidents of violence. Safety representatives should also be consulted (see chapter 15); they can help you to develop the organisation's policy. Clearly the organisation cannot guard against all eventualities, nor can action by the employer alone bring the problem under control. But to minimise the threat of violence, it is very important to discuss the results with all staff and volunteers – any policy which is not jointly developed by staff and volunteers is unlikely to have their support or commitment and will be less effective.

Step 1 – Look for the hazard

You could develop a questionnaire with staff, volunteers (and the safety representative, if available) to determine the potential for violence in your workplace.

Step 2 – Decide who might be harmed, and how

Who are, or could be, potentially at risk from threats or violence?

Step 3 – Evaluate the risks arising from the hazards and decide whether existing control measures are adequate or if more should be done

If a problem has been identified, look for ways to reduce the threat of violence. For instance, you could ensure that people work in pairs, or train your personnel in how to recognise potentially violent situations and equip them to defuse such situations.

Step 1	Look for the hazard.
Step 2	Decide who might be harmed, and how.
Step 3	Evaluate the risks arising from the hazard and decide whether existing control measures are adequate or if more should be done.
Step 4	Record your findings and insert these into your health and safety management document. Inform all staff and volunteers.
Step 5	Review your assessment from time to time and make changes if necessary.

Set up a formal reporting system to investigate incidents of threats and violence.

Step 4 – Record your findings and insert these into your health and safety management document. Inform all staff and volunteers

Your findings should be recorded; this will help you to address any problems which may arise in the future.

Step 5 – Review your assessment from time to time and make changes if necessary

Investigate with staff and volunteers any reported incidents of violence. Ensure that these investigations are used in developing policies to prevent incidents from re-occurring. Policies on preventing or dealing with violence should be reviewed regularly to check their effectiveness.

Further advice

Don't go over the top. The HSE in its leaflet 'Violence to Staff' recommends trying to balance the risks to your employees against any possible side effects on the public. An atmosphere that suggests employees are worried about violence can sometimes increase the likelihood of it happening.

We have included forms for your use to record violent incidents – you may wish to adapt the forms for your group.

Don't forget: your clients may be vulnerable too – from their relatives, friends, neighbours, volunteers or even your own staff members. However, this book is primarily concerned about the health and safety of staff and voluntary members of groups. We advise any group working with vulnerable clients to refer to the following publications:

♦ 'Safe and Alert: Good practice advice on volunteers working with vulnerable clients', NCVO Publications

♦ 'Inter-Agency Procedures: Abuse of older people in domestic settings', Consumer, Carer & Public Information Unit, Liverpool (tel: 0151 225 3927)

♦ 'Personal Safety for Health Care Workers', P. Bibby, commissioned by the Suzy Lamplugh Trust, Arena 1995

For further information contact the Suzy Lamplugh Trust at: 14 East Sheen Avenue, London SW14 8AS Tel: 020 8392 1839.

When you have completed this chapter, turn to the checklist on page 65 and tick off the actions you have taken.

VIOLENCE QUESTIONNAIRE

Male [ ] 1   Volunteer [ ] 3   Age [ ] 5 yrs

Female [ ] 2   Staff member [ ] 4

What job(s) do you do? _____ 6   Number of hours a week _____ 7

Start time _____ 8 a.m./p.m.   Finish time _____ 9 a.m./p.m.

Do you consider the problem of violence or the threat of violence in your organisation to be

very serious [ ] 10   minor [ ] 12

serious [ ] 11   non-existent [ ] 13

Have you ever felt threatened in your work for this organisation?

never [ ] 14   more than once [ ] 16

once [ ] 15   often [ ] 17

If yes, under what circumstances? _____ 18

How long have you worked with us?

[ ] 19 less than 1 year   [ ] 20 1–2 years   [ ] 21 more than 2 years

What is your ethnic origin?

[ ] 22 white   [ ] 23 black/African   [ ] 24 black/Caribbean   [ ] 25 black/other

[ ] 26 Pakistani   [ ] 27 Indian   [ ] 28 Bangladeshi   [ ] 29 Chinese

[ ] 30 Irish   [ ] 31 other _____

Do you consider yourself to have a disability?   [ ] Yes [ ] No 32

Are you registered disabled?   [ ] Yes [ ] No 33

Briefly describe the activities you do _____

_____

_____ 34

Have you any suggestions or comments about the issues raised in this questionnaire? _____

_____

_____

_____ 35

SUPERVISOR'S REPORT

Name _____   Date form completed _____

I have read the report by _____
and have taken the following action _____
_____
_____

I recommend the following action _____
_____
_____

Sick leave taken by member of staff/volunteer involved _____

RIDDOR form completed _____

Name of assailant _____   Sex: ☐ M   ☐ F

Known to the organisation?   ☐ Yes   ☐ No

Address _____
_____
_____

POLICE INVOLVEMENT

Incident reported to the police?   ☐ Yes   ☐ No

Charges made _____

Details _____
_____
_____

ORGANISATION RESPONSE

Action to be taken _____
_____
_____

Entry to be made in the accident book _____
_____
_____

Signed _____   Date _____

INCIDENT FORM FOR STAFF AND VOLUNTEERS

If the person involved in the incident is not capable of filling in this form, a senior member of staff or member of the governing body should complete the form, giving relevant details as known.

NB: The person involved in the incident should fill in an incident form as soon as possible.

Block capitals please (don't worry about spelling or grammar)

Date of incident _____   Time _____   Date form completed _____

Name of person involved in incident _____

Role in organisation _____

☐ Full-time   ☐ Part-time

Ethnicity_____

How long in organisation?   Years _____   months _____

Location at which incident occurred _____

☐ On duty   ☐ Off duty

What was the person involved in the incident doing at the time?_____

_____

Type of incident (you may tick more than one box)

☐ A. Verbal threat

☐ B. Severe verbal abuse

☐ C. Racial

☐ D. Threatening posture

☐ E. Threat with weapon

☐ F. Sexual

☐ G. Physical assault

☐ H. Attempted theft

☐ I. Other (please specify) _____

Give an account in your own words of what happened and any relevant incidents leading to the incident. Attach a separate sheet if necessary.

_____

_____

Please include any details of any furniture or other items which may have been used in a threatening manner or were actually used in the incident.

_____

_____

Nature and extent of injuries (list all physical injuries sustained, including cuts and bruises)

_____
_____
_____

Emotional effects

_____
_____
_____

Damage to personal property, including clothing

_____
_____
_____

Treatment given for injuries

_____
_____
_____

Given by _____

Treated in hospital _____

Date _____

Name of person who alerted staff to incident _____

How long after the incident occurred? _____

Name(s) of any witnesses

Name _____ Occupation _____

Address if not working in organisation _____
_____
_____

Name of person recording incident _____

Address if not working in organisation _____
_____
_____

Signed _____   Date _____

Chapter 10
Stress

In a sector which is non-profit-making and which prides itself on its caring and altruistic nature, it might be thought that stess is not a serious problem. However, in a poll of 600 London-based voluntary organisations carried out between February and June 2000, 85% identified work stress as their major health and safety issue. This could indicate that the sector does not take as much care of its staff and volunteers as it would like to believe.

Health effects linked to stress (including anxiety and depression) are estimated to account for a third of sickness absence in the UK, and in 1995 the Department of Health estimated that 91 million working days are lost each year due to stress-related illness – at a cost of £3.7 billion.

Furthermore, in the TUC's 'Annual Survey of Trade Union Health and Safety Representatives 2000' 82% of health and safety representatives working in the voluntary sector reported that work stress is their primary concern. A study on the effects of stress in 1999 concluded that stress is an issue for the voluntary sector in Merseyside, while anecdotal evidence indicates that the levels in the sector are rising.

Stress is very often misunderstood, so in this chapter we are going to review:

1 What is stress?
2 What can cause stress in an organisation?
3 How to recognise if your organisation has a problem with stress
4 How to minimise the effects of stress
5 Helping those who have been effected by stress

1 What is stress?

According to a booklet produced by the Health and Safety Executive on the subject: 'Stress is people's natural reaction to excessive pressure, it isn't a disease. But if stress is excessive and goes on for some time, it can lead to mental and physical ill health (e.g. depression, nervous breakdown, heart disease).'

Each of us reacts to challenges in our own way, and a situation easily dealt with by one person could cause a lot of difficulties for someone else. This may be due to differences in personality, age, experience or training. For example, a 17-year-old with no financial commitments may be less affected by work pressure than a 38-year-old single parent with two young children, balancing home life with work. Equally, some circumstances may present more of a challenge to the younger person, who may lack relevant experience.

It is important to remember that our individual capacities to deal with situations vary, depending on what else is happening in our lives. Sometimes events and pressures from home can add to pressure at work; for instance, a bereavement may affect our ability to cope. It can also work the other way round, when events at work make home life more difficult; for example, working long or unsociable hours can lead to arguments and relationship problems at home.

A young volunteer was put on a charity's telephone helpline without training and was immediately inundated with telephone enquiries she could not answer. She felt very insecure, has lost confidence and plans not to return to the charity.

Stress often occurs when individuals experience an overload of demand, particularly when they have little control over work and cannot choose how to deal with it. This can alter the way they think and behave, which may make them less able to deal with the pressures. Others may become stressed by too little stimulation: boring and repetitive work can also lead to problems.

Don't forget: anyone can suffer the effects of stress, whatever the job. It is not a sign of weakness – in fact, it may take more strength to admit your vulnerability and ask for help.

Possible signs that an individual is affected by stress are:

♦ increased absenteeism;
♦ poor punctuality;
♦ gain or loss of weight;
♦ increased intake of stimulants (such as coffee, cigarettes, alcohol);
♦ withdrawal from social interaction;
♦ indecisiveness;
♦ reduced effectiveness;
♦ tiredness and lethargy.

Note: these are just a few of the possible symptoms – their presence does not automatically imply that the person is affected by stress.

2 What can cause high levels of stress in an organisation?

Causes of organisational stress are many and varied, and may affect each organisation differently. We list here a selection of factors which may cause stress, or increase the levels of stress within an organisation.

Workplace environment

♦ poor standards of health and safety;
♦ unsatisfactory working environment (for instance, inappropriate temperature, lighting, ventilation, noise levels, amount of space);
♦ using inappropriate or old equipment;
♦ workplace in poor general repair.

Job structure

♦ inappropriate amount of work (too much or too little);
♦ ambiguous or conflicting roles;
♦ poorly designed shift patterns;
♦ long or unsociable hours;
♦ lack of control;
♦ poor promotion prospects;
♦ short-term contracts;
♦ low wages;
♦ insufficient training.

Organisational culture

♦ competitive;
♦ bullying;
♦ aggressive;
♦ no involvement of staff when dealing with constant change;
♦ unsupportive;
♦ tendency to blame others;
♦ unreasonable expectations;
♦ poor management;
♦ ineffective trustees.

Nature of work

♦ dealing with aggressive or violent clients;
♦ constant change;
♦ insecure funding leading to job insecurity.

Inter-personal support

♦ low perceived value of work;
♦ excessive responsibility without support;
♦ lack of appreciation from managers and/or clients;
♦ lack of support (such as insensitive management or trustees, conflict with colleagues).

Some of the points listed above can have a cumulative effect, as in the example below.

> A person working for a children's charity may well feel that it is worthwhile putting up with an interfering trustee, low pay and old equipment in return for the satisfaction of helping the children. However, the situation may well change if the office heating fails – this could be the last straw.

3 How to recognise if your organisation has a problem with stress

Stop, question and listen

As discussed above, stress affects different people in different ways, and so it may not be immediately obvious whether stress is a problem in your organisation.

Some issues to consider:

- Have you asked staff or volunteers how they feel about the job?
- Do you have a regular appraisal system in place?
- Do staff and volunteers feel able to talk to members of the governing body?
- Have you examined the level of sickness absence of staff or volunteers?
- Do you have a high turnover of personnel?
- Are people aggressive or uncooperative?
- Is there tension or conflict between people working for the organisation?

If you suspect that stress caused or made worse by work could affect the health of people involved in your organisation, your first step should be to carry out a risk assessment. The same method outlined in chapter 5 can be used for stress (see table below).

You should look on the risk assessment process as a positive course of action. If your organisation makes an effort to understand what affects the performance of your staff and volunteers, it is more likely to be able to prevent health problems linked to excessive stress. Benefits to the organisation could be reduced staff turnover, more effective work performance and lower absenteeism.

Stress survey

You may wish to combine your risk assessment with a simple survey. This can be a useful way of gathering data from everyone involved in the organisation, without anyone being identified. It can also be effective in providing potential solutions for some of the problems identified. Try to provide space for people to say what they

Step 1	Look for the hazard. (For instance, look for pressures at work which could cause long-lasting levels of stress.)
Step 2	Decide who might be harmed, and how.
Step 3	Evaluate the risks arising from the hazard and decide whether existing control measures are adequate or if more should be done. (This step should involve talking to people to determine how they feel about their jobs, as individuals need different levels of support at different times.)
Step 4	Record your findings and insert these into your health and safety management document. Inform all staff and volunteers.
Step 5	Review your assessment from time to time and make changes if necessary.

enjoy about the work, or ask about procedures already in place which are thought to be effective, so that the positive aspects of the organisation can be appreciated too.

In a very small organisation, it may be difficult to ensure confidentiality and individuals may feel that they could be identified from their responses. To get around this, you could ask an independent colleague from another charity to collate the data from the questionnaires. In very large organisations, you could choose to select a sample of the staff and/or volunteers, rather than involve everyone. Make sure that you involve representatives of all types of work undertaken by the organisation, including those who may work part-time, such as cleaners. Another possibility is to set up focus groups to obtain a general understanding of the key issues.

Alternatively, it may be more practical to call a meeting and chat to staff and volunteers about the issues (or establish focus groups in larger organisations) – including members of the governing body and/or users, if appropriate. You need to find out whether people would be comfortable discussing these matters in a group – if people are feeling stressed and disempowered, will they feel they can be honest? Don't forget that in some cases bullying can be very subtle, and you may not be aware of tensions between personnel. There may be other factors, such as cultural ones, which need to be considered here as well.

It is a good idea to involve staff and volunteers in the development of the survey, or the planning of the meeting, to ensure that all relevant points are included. Set a timetable for various stages of the process, including when targets will be achieved, and keep people informed. Don't forget to consult with the safety representative or trade union representative if your organisation has one – they may also be aware of action taken in other organisations which could give some guidance to your organisation.

Be careful not to raise expectations that cannot be met – try to ensure that the process is supported by as many members of the organisation as possible, so that there is some commitment to making necessary changes. But also remember that it may take some time before measurable change is seen. Don't forget to review the situation after a reasonable amount of time has passed, to see if progress has been made and to identify any new problems that may have arisen.

You may wish to start this process in-house, but then decide that you would benefit from some independent help and support from outside the organisation. Some sources of advice and guidance are listed at the end of this chapter.

4 How to minimise the effects of high levels of stress

If you find evidence of stress caused by the organisation, you are legally bound as an employer to make changes to alleviate the situation for paid staff. You also have a duty of care towards volunteers and others associated with you organisation (see chapter 1). It is a good idea to develop policies and procedures to make sure that you address the issue of stress in a systematic and effective manner. In summary, this involves preventing stress by addressing its root causes; minimising its effects by training and appropriate management, and providing support to those affected by it. (The booklet 'Mental Health in the Workplace', by the Mental Health Foundation, discusses developing a policy for mental health at work in more detail – see page 49 for information.)

You may not be able to change everything at once, but you can set some achievable goals – small successes can help to motivate everyone to address more difficult issues. A great deal of progress can be made without spending a lot of money – do not let your organisation use lack of resources as an excuse for avoiding change.

You may be able to seek help from your local Council of Voluntary Services (CVS), as it is

In one organisation, the risk assessment identified that a number of care workers were concerned about visiting clients who had a history of physical violence. A solution was found by agreeing a contract of behaviour with the client and their family. The contract recognised that clients were vulnerable, but also laid down clear guidelines on what was considered to be acceptable behaviour, and what was unacceptable, as a condition of support. The contract was borrowed and adopted from an organisation which supported similar clients.

likely that other organisations have faced similar problems in the past and found ways to deal with them.

Possible changes which may help to alleviate high levels of stress

- rearranging workloads;
- reducing responsibility by delegating work;
- reviewing training needs;
- addressing concerns about the workplace environment (such as temperature);
- encouraging people to take their lunch breaks away from the workplace;
- developing family-friendly policies;
- arranging regular team meetings;
- ensuring that the views of staff and volunteers are heard;
- adopting flexi-time arrangements;

The workload of an office administrator was constantly being increased and his supervisor was very scathing and critical about his inability to finish work on time. The administrator was feeling very threatened and undermined. After the survey, which was carried out as part of the risk assessment, it was found that several people had identified similar problems with the supervisor. The supervisor was shocked that people felt threatened by her behaviour. She was sent on a relatively inexpensive training course recommended by the Directory of Social Change. A new survey will take place in six months' time to review progress in the whole organisation.

- reviewing job descriptions – check that they reflect current roles and responsibilities;
- paying volunteers reasonable expenses, and on time.

5 Helping those who have been affected by stress

Individual approaches

Remember that mechanisms to improve individual coping skills may be helpful for some people, especially in the short term, but you must tackle the root cause of stress in the workplace.

Arrange for training to improve personal coping skills

Training courses vary in quality and cost. They normally teach people how to cope on an individual level with stress, and may include breathing exercises, time management and other forms of coping skills.

Set up counselling sessions

Counselling sessions provide individuals with the opportunity to talk privately about their problems and how to deal with them. This may well cover issues both inside and outside the workplace.

Encourage staff and/or volunteers to take regular exercise

Regular exercise has been found to help individuals cope with high levels of stress.

Employing people with mental health problems

Stress is becoming increasingly common in our society, yet there is a stigma attached to anyone who is affected (or has been affected) by stress or any other form of mental ill health. Greater acceptance of mental distress is needed, together with an acknowledgement that it can affect everyone at some time in their lives. The Disability Discrimination Act 1995 may help to improve this acceptance and to prevent discrimination against those who have been affected by mental ill health, for example during recruitment or selection procedures and in other areas of employment (see chapter 12).

Advice and guidance

Since the publication of this book the Health and Safety Executive have published Management Standards for Work Related Stress. Information and guidelines can be obtained from: www.hse.gov.uk/stress/standards/ or by telephone on 0845 345 00.

General advice is available from:

◆ Health @ Work, Ground Floor, Orleans House, Edmund Street, Liverpool, L3 9NG (tel: 0151 236 6608)
◆ HSE Infoline, a confidential phone service (tel: 08701 545500)
◆ HSE website: www.hsedirect.com
◆ Your local Environmental Health Services Department (the number will be in your local phone book)
◆ Your local CVS – contact details available from the National Association of Councils for Voluntary Service, Arundel Court, 177 Arundel Street, Sheffield S1 2NU (tel: 0114 278 6635)

◆ Health Development Agency, Trevelyan House, 30 Great Peter Street, London SW1 2HW (tel: 020 7413 1991)
◆ Mental Health Foundation, 20–21 Cornwall Terrace, London NW1 4QL (tel: 020 7535 7400)
◆ UK National Work Stress Network, 9 Bell Lane, Syresham, Brackley NN13 5HP (tel: 01280 850 388; e-mail: la-n66@nasuwt.org.uk

Advice on choosing external consultants is available from:

◆ British Psychological Society, St Andrews House, Leicester LE1 7DR (tel: 0116 254 9568)

Useful publications

◆ 'Tackling Work-related Stress: A guide for employees'. HSE Books 2001 (INDG341; ISBN 0 7176 2500)
◆ 'Mental Health in the Workplace: Tackling the effects of stress', Mental Health Foundation 2000 (ISBN 0 901944 84 X)
◆ 'Tackling Work-related Stress: A manager's guide', HSE Books 2001 (ISBN 0 7176 0506)
◆ 'Mental Well-being in the Workplace: A resource pack for management training and development: HSE Books 1998 (ISBN 0 7176 1524 3)

When you have completed this chapter, turn to the checklist on page 65 and tick off the actions you have taken.

Chapter 11
First aid

All employers have a duty under the law to provide first aid facilities and equipment that are adequate and appropriate for each workplace.

By law,[1] employers must:
- make an assessment to decide what first aid facilities are adequate and appropriate for your organisation, which is done by making an assessment;
- provide adequate equipment and facilities.

For instance, an organisation that refurbishes old gas ovens and fridges will have different first aid requirements from those of an organisation offering computer training to the unemployed. This is why an assessment needs to be carried out, and why the regulations do not give a definitive list of requirments, except for outlining the minimum standards that all organisations have to achieve.

Carrying out a first aid assessment

Some factors to be considered:
- Workplace hazards and risks. For instance, are any dangerous chemicals or machinery being used?
- The size of the organisation. The more personnel you have, the greater the risk of someone needing first aid.
- The organisation's history of accidents.
- The nature and distribution of the workforce. (Do personnel work alone or in remote areas?)
- The nature of activities. For example, the assessment of an organisation that takes parties of young children canoeing will be very different from that of an organisation

arranging school trips to the theatre. If minibuses are used, are first aid kits fitted? Are personnel trained to administer first aid?
- The availability of emergency medical services. (Some countryside organisations work in very remote locations.)
- Employees working in shared or multi-occupied sites. It is very easy to assume that the business or organisation next door will have a first aid kit or a first aider
- Holiday and other absences. These may leave your organisation with no first aiders and/or appointed persons (see below for definitions).

Assessment is the key to all of these issues (see also chapter 5).

Results of the assessment

After you have completed your first aid assessment, you can use the results obtained to decide on the type of first aid provision you need and the number of first aiders or appointed persons required. Don't forget, you should make sure any provision takes into account the working patterns of your organisation, as well as periods of holiday or sick leave.

A first aider is someone who has completed a first aid course of at least 24 hours, approved by the Health and Safety Executive (normally carried out over four days).

An appointed person is someone who has basic first aid knowledge and is available whenever people are at work. They can take charge in an emergency and are responsible for calling the emergency services. One-day courses are available to train appointed persons.

Remember that a trained first aider is an asset to any organisation.

---

1 *The Health and Safety (First Aid) Regulations 1981.*

Training

First aiders have to be re-trained within three years of their last training. You should keep records of the relevant training and re-training dates. The training should be provided by organisations approved by the Health and Safety Executive.

Free help and advice on all matters relating to first aid are available from the Health and Safety Executive. It may also have information concerning local first aid approved courses.

First aid equipment

The assessment will also determine what first aid equipment is required.

There must be at least one first aid box, which should be in a readily accessible location and properly equipped.

First aid provision should be readily available to each employee and volunteer at all times and they must be informed of its location. Don't forget the times when people are driving – it is good practice to ensure that all vehicles

used for your organisation's activities have a first aid box.

There is no mandatory list of contents for a first aid box – contents vary, depending on the information gathered during the assessment of first aid needs. As a guide, where no special risk arises in the workplace, a minimum stock of first aid items would normally be:

- a leaflet giving general guidance on first aid (for example, an HSE leaflet);[2]
- 20 individually wrapped sterile adhesive dressings (assorted sizes), appropriate to the type of work;
- two sterile eye pads;
- four individually wrapped triangular bandages (preferably sterile);
- six safety pins (not appropriate in certain organisations, for example when dealing with childcare or food preparation);
- six medium-sized individually wrapped sterile unmedicated wound dressings – approximately 12cm x 12cm (about 5in x 5in);
- two large sterile individually wrapped unmedicated wound dressings – approximately 18cm x 18cm (about 7in x 7in);
- one pair of disposable gloves.

 Volunteers only

The need to provide first aid facilities and equipment for voluntary and community based activities is covered by the general duty of care (see chapter 1).

Organisations with volunteers only should always first undertake an assessment of the first aid needs of their organisation. For instance, an organisation that organises cricket games would not need the same first aid facilities as one that organises mountain climbing expeditions.

Examples of assessments could be:
- for coffee mornings, an organisation decided that no trained first aider was required but that an appointed person should be available;
- for a large car boot sale, a trained first aider was provided;
- for a fireworks display, trained first aiders, a rest tent and an ambulance were required;
- for renovation and building work carried out by volunteers, a trained first aider was required;
- for volunteers doing domestic gardening, an appointed person and a mobile first aid box were provided.

Remember that although generally it may not be compulsory for all voluntary organisations to have a trained first aid person, they are an asset to any group. Taking the steps above and implementing the results will go a long way towards demonstrating to your volunteers the value that your organisation places on them. It will also help you to feel confident that your first aid needs are being met.

---

2 *'Basic Advice on First Aid at Work' IND(G)215L, HSE Books 1997 (ISBN 0 7176 1070 5)*

There must be at least one notice telling employees:

- the location of the first aid box;
- the identity of the first aider or appointed person;
- the location of the first aider or appointed person.

If the workplace gives rise to special hazards, such as using a particularly toxic material, then a trained first aider may be needed. If you are in any doubt about this, ask. Help is available from your EHSD or the HSE.

When you have completed this chapter, turn to the checklist on page 65 and tick off the actions you have taken.

Chapter 12
Individuals with specific needs

Certain individuals have needs which are specific and should be considered when developing policies and procedures for health and safety. Any risk assessment that you carry out should be thorough in considering the needs of people who will or may be involved in your organisation's activities, but we have outlined some particular examples below.

Pregnant women[1]

The needs of new and expectant mothers must be included in the risk assessment (see the Management of Health and Safety at Work Regulations 1999). The Regulations now specifically require employers to pay particular attention to risks that could affect the health and safety of expectant or new mothers, and their babies.

Pregnant workers are especially at risk from manual handling activities – for example, hormonal changes can affect the ligaments, increasing susceptibility to injury, while postural problems may increase as the pregnancy progresses. Other potential risks include long working hours, unrealistic targets and lack of control over the work, which may lead to stress.

Children and young persons

Children
Childcare
Any activity involving children has to be given special attention regarding safety. Legislation is

in place (including the Children's Act 1989 and the Child Protection Act 1990) which imposes duties on those who undertake a caring role.

You should consult your local Social Services Department regarding any childcare activity that you take on. Registration of anyone working with children (including volunteers) is now dealt with by the Criminal Records Bureau (situated at your local Passport Office – your local library, Citizens Advice Bureau or phone book will have contact details), rather than the police authority.

Restrictions on the employment of children
For employment purposes the following definitions apply: a child is someone under the school leaving age of 16 years, and a young person is someone under the age of 18.

No child under the age of 13 can be employed in any capacity, and no child between the ages of 13 and 16 can be employed during school hours, before 7a.m. and after 7.p.m. on any day, for more than two hours on any school day, or for more than two hours on Sunday.

The work of 13- to 16-year-olds can be controlled by local authority bye-laws, so check before you enter into any employment situation.

Information given to parents about health risks
Before their child undertakes any employment, parents must be given information on the assessed health and safety risks of the employment, and the preventive and protective measures you propose to undertake.

Young persons
The Management of Health and Safety at Work Regulations 1999 include risk assessments involving the employment of any young person,

---

1 'Maternity Rights – a guide for employers and employees' DTI/HSE PL958(Rev2).

which must be carried out before they start work. You must take into account the following:

- the inexperience, lack of awareness and immaturity of the young person;
- the layout of the workplace;
- any exposure to dangerous physical, chemical and biological agents;
- the work equipment;
- the processes and activities;
- health and safety training;
- specific agents and processes.[2]

Monitoring

Where the assessment shows that there is a risk to the safety, physical or mental health or development of the young person, then health monitoring must be provided on a regular basis.

Information for employees

Young people employed must be given comprehensive information on:

- the risks to health and safety identified by the risk assessment;
- the preventive and protective measures adopted;
- the emergency procedures to be followed in the event of dangerous situations;
- the identity of those persons who have responsibility for implementing emergency procedures;
- other risks that are present in the workplace caused by other employers sharing the workplace.

Disabled staff

The Disability Discrimination Act 1995 introduced new laws and measures aimed at ending the discrimination that many disabled people face in their day-to-day lives. The employment provision of the Act (Disability Discrimination (Employment) Regulations 1996), which came into force on 2 December 1996, is an attempt to protect people with disabilities, and those who have been disabled, from discrimination in the area of employment.

All employers with more than 15 staff have to take measures to avoid discriminating against disabled persons and have to make necessary changes in order to 'reasonably accommodate' such workers in their business.

Disabled people are a valuable and untapped resource in our society, and charities and voluntary groups have a particular duty to avoid treating people with disabilities in a discriminatory manner.

Employers have to make 'reasonable adjustments' if their employment arrangements or premises place disabled people at a substantial disadvantage compared with non-disabled people.

What might be a reasonable adjustment?

For example, if you do not recruit someone who uses a wheelchair because the work station is inaccessible to people in wheelchairs, this would be seen as less favourable treatment arising from a reason relating to the disability if someone else who did not have an accessibility problem was (or would have been) recruited instead. You could not justify that treatment of the disabled job applicant if, for instance, a simple rearrangement of the furniture would have eased access. In short, if you could easily have adjusted the office (or made some other reasonable adjustment) but did not do so, then you might lose an industrial tribunal case arising from such circumstances.

The Act also makes it unlawful for an employer to discriminate against a disabled person for a reason which relates to their disability in respect of selection, recruitment, promotion, training or terms of employment, including benefits and working conditions.

Example 1

An employer shortlisting applicants for a junior office position is considering whether or not to

2 Refer to the Health and Safety (Young Persons) Regulations 1997.

include a blind applicant whom the employer believes might present a safety risk while moving around a crowded office space. A 'reasonable adjustment' might be to provide mobility training to familiarise the new employee with the work area, so removing any risk there might otherwise be.[3]

However, in a recent case a visually impaired man was turned down for a job interview because he could not drive. His case was taken to an industrial tribunal under the Disability Discrimination Act 1995. The case fell at the first hurdle because the Act covers only employers with more than 20 employees, whereas the organisation had just 14 staff and over 20 volunteers. However, the organisation admitted that it had failed to consider the possibility of alternative transport or additional financial assistance.

The Act also outlaws discrimination by providers of services such as doctors or dentists, providers of goods such as shops and restaurants, and people or organisations which offer facilities such as libraries and museums. If your organisation provides services, you should already have considered how the Act may affect your work practices and work environment.

You can treat a disabled person less favourably only if you reasonably believe that either the disabled customer or someone else may come to some harm if you do not do so. Your reasons for providing less favourable treatment must be genuine in these circumstances.

Example 2
A wheelchair user with a back injury wants to work out by using the weights in a gym. The supervisor believes the customer would be at risk of injuring herself. However, if (for example) the disabled customer informs him that there is no risk because her doctor has advised her that exercising will not strain her back, the supervisor must be ready to change his mind.[4]

This section can only briefly cover the Act and you are advised to seek further information from:

◆ Disability on the Agenda, Freepost, London SE99 7EQ
  (tel: 0345 622 633; textphone: 0345 622 644)
◆ DDA Information, Freepost MID02164, Stratford-upon-Avon, CV37 9BR
  (helpline: 0345 622633)

When you have completed this chapter, turn to the checklist on page 65 and tick off the actions you have taken.

---

3 *This example is taken from The Disability Discrimination Act (What Employers Need to Know). Available from DDA Information.*
4 *This example is taken from The Disability Discrimination Act (What Service Providers Need to Know). Available from DDA Information.*

Chapter 13
Food hygiene

The supply of food and drinks is a common activity in the majority of voluntary organisations, both for providing refreshments to members and for fundraising events. The requirement to provide food and drink that are safe is absolute; any person falling ill as a result of your culinary activities may be able to seek damages if you have been negligent. There is a general duty of care to provide wholesome, safe food and drink in all circumstances, for instance on a camping trip or at a barbecue. If you are supplying food as an organisation or as an individual on behalf of an organisation, whether for sale or free of charge, you have to comply with the regulations below.

Illness and deaths due to food poisoning have been given a high media profile in recent years. The Food Standards Agency, set up in April 2000, is now the governing body on food issues.

Here we have included the main requirements of the Food Safety Act 1990 as well as various regulations. Throughout the regulations the word 'food' includes drink for human consumption, including alcoholic drinks.

The Food Safety Act 1990 requires that food for human consumption is safe and not falsely labelled or presented. There are other regulations regarding food hygiene made under this Act, and the three component areas of these which may apply to voluntary organisations are outlined below.

1 The Food Safety (General Food Hygiene) Regulations 1995

These create the basic framework for food hygiene law, specifying the basic hygiene conditions for food businesses. These regulations apply to food which is produced commercially for profit as well as to food produced by voluntary groups or any other non-profit-making organisation.

The persons in charge must ensure that:
- food handlers are supervised and trained in food hygiene matters;
- those in charge of food production control the quality of the food by good management of hygiene.

The regulations also require that:
- people handling food maintain the correct standards of personal hygiene;
- sanitary facilities and wash basins are provided;
- the work area and equipment are clean;
- suitable premises are provided;
- there are suitable arrangements for food waste;
- there are proper arrangements for moveable or temporary premises, including transport – for example, check that the site is suitable, and that the water supply is wholesome and without risk.

2 The Food Safety (Temperature Control) Regulations 1995

These specify the temperatures at which foods must be kept. Generally speaking, food which can support bacterial growth must be kept refrigerated at a temperature of 5°C, served at a temperature of at least 65°C and stored in a freezer at −18°C. You should record the temperature on the gauges of fridges and hot plates daily.

3 The Food Premises (Registration) Regulations 1991

These require that food premises (including vehicles) be registered with the local authority, in order that the premises can be inspected. Organisations dealing with food must register with the local authority (usually the EHSD) if their premises are used on five or more consecutive days or if they are used on more than five days in any five consecutive weeks. A maximum fine of £1,000 can be imposed for failing to register with the local authority, so you are well advised to check.

The Food Safety Act 1990 and the regulations allow a defence of due diligence. Here the defendant needs to show that they took all reasonable precautions; records of systems of control, training records, cleaning regimes and risk assessments will need to be evident.

If catering is a regular activity there will be a need for key personnel who handle food (including volunteers) to attend a basic Food and Hygiene Certificate course. For details of such a course in your area, contact your local EHSD.

When you have completed this chapter, turn to the checklist on page 65 and tick off the actions you have taken.

Chapter 14

Recording and reporting of sickness, incidents and accidents

The recording of accidents and incidents in your organisation is an essential part of any health and safety procedure, even if there is no injury, and however many employees or volunteers you may have. By investigating and recording all accidents and incidents, you can identify any action that should be taken to prevent further accidents. It is also a good idea to record and investigate all 'near misses' – today's near miss could be tomorrow's accident.

By law:

- All workplaces with more than 10 employees, and all factories, must have an accident book where details of all accidents can be recorded.
- The book should also be used to record any sickness that was possibly caused or made worse by work, and any dangerous occurrences or 'near misses' in the workplace.
- Accident book entries must be 'torn off' and stored in compliance with the Data Protection Act 1998. Records should be kept for at least three years after the last entry.

 Volunteers Only

For all organisations, it is good practice to record any accidents, incidents or near misses in order to identify any action which would help to prevent a similar event occurring again.

Organisations with volunteers only, and which do not own premises, are not bound by the RIDDOR regulations, but they are required to inform their insurance company of any incident or accident, and obviously any major injury or death must be reported to the emergency authorities.

An example of a form suitable for recording minor incidents is provided at the end of the chapter. The form in your health and safety policy can be used as your accident and incident book.

The Reporting of Injuries, Diseases and Dangerous Occurrences Regulations 1995 (RIDDOR)

If you are an employer, self-employed or in control of work premises, you are required under RIDDOR to report some work-related accidents, diseases and dangerous occurrences.

It is a legal requirement to report accidents and ill health. This information enables the Health and Safety Executive (HSE) and local authorities to identify where and how risks arise and to investigate serious accidents.

The following MUST be reported:

- a death or major injury;
- an 'over three-day' injury (i.e. one that results in the injured person being unable to work for more than three days)
- a work-related disease;
- a dangerous occurrence.

(Note that any injury which results in a member of the public being taken to hospital is also reportable.)

What's new?

In order to comply with the Data Protection Act 1998 (DPA), from 31st December 2003 it is essential that all personal details entered into accident books are kept confidential. With this in mind a new accident book has been introduced which meets all of the requirements of DPA.

The new HSE accident book incorporates perforated slips that can be removed following completion and stored securely. It enables employers to keep personal information confidential and ensures that they are compliant with the following legislation:
♦ Social Security Act (Claims and Payments) Regulations 1979
♦ Health and Safety at Work etc. Act 1974
♦ Social Security Administration Act 1992
♦ Reporting of Diseases and Dangersous Occurrences Regulations (RIDDOR) 1995
♦ Data Protection Act (DPA) 1998.

Copies of the HSE accident book price can be purchased from:
HSE books PO Box 1999, Sudbury, Suffolk CO10 2WA; tel: 01787 881165

The reporting procedure, which has been in place since 1996, has been simplified and offers a facility to report all cases to a single point – the Incident Contact Centre (ICC), based at Caerphilly in Wales.

This new arrangement has been available since 1 April 2001. The centre means that you no longer need to be concerned about which office you need to report to.

Incidents can be reported in a variety of ways:
♦ by phone;
♦ by fax;
♦ via the internet;
♦ or by post.

You should report incidents via the quickest way (usually by phone), and then send forms by one of the other methods within 10 days.

The telephone service is available Monday to Friday between the hours of 8.30a.m. and 5p.m. Tel: 0845 300 9923; fax: 0845 300 9924.

Postal address (for reports): Incident Contact Centre, Caerphilly Business Park, Caerphilly, CF83 3GG

E-mail: riddor@natbrit.com

For internet reports go to: www.riddor.gov.uk Or alternatively link in via the HSE website at: www.hse.gov.uk

Further information

'Guide to the Reporting of Injuries, Diseases and Dangerous Occurrences Regulations 1995: Guidance on regulations L73', 1999 (HSE Books ISBN 0 7176 2431 5)

'RIDDOR Explained: The reporting of injuries, diseases and dangerous occurrences regulations', HSE31 (rev. 1) 1999 (ISBN 0 7176 2441 2). Free leaflet, also available in packs of 10.

When you have completed this chapter, turn to the checklist on page 65 and tick off the actions you have taken.

INCIDENT FORM

NB: This form is NOT a RIDDOR form, but it is one way to record incidents. You could design your own form, or use a notebook.

GENERAL DETAILS OF INCIDENT

Date of incident _____

Exact location of incident _____

Is the organisation in overall control of the premises/event? ☐ Yes ☐ No

If no, give the name of the owner/leaseholder _____

INJURED PERSON

Full name _____

Age _____ Sex: ☐ M ☐ F

Address _____

_____

Nature of injury (state left or right as appropriate) _____

_____

Status of injured person (tick as appropriate)

☐ employee of organisation   ☐ employee of another organisation
☐ self-employed person   ☐ member of public
☐ volunteer (includes members of governing body) ☐ person being cared for by organisation
☐ contractor   ☐ other

ROLE IN ORGANISATION

How long with organisation _____ years _____ months

What was the injured person doing at the time of the incident? _____

Was this something they were authorised to do? ☐ Yes ☐ No

Were they authorised to be where the incident occurred? ☐ Yes ☐ No

When was the incident reported to you? _____ date _____ time

Was the incident witnessed by someone else ☐ Yes ☐ No

Was first aid treatment given on site? ☐ Yes ☐ No Details _____

Was hospital/medical treatment obtained? ☐ Yes ☐ No Details _____

Anticipated absence from organisation ☐ no time lost ☐ less than 3 days ☐ 3 days or more

FURTHER DETAILS OF INCIDENT _____

_____

List training requirements to prevent re-occurrence _____

_____

Does a RIDDOR form need to be completed? ☐ Yes ☐ No

If yes, has it been sent in? ☐ Yes ☐ No

Comments _____

_____

Signed _____ Date _____

Chapter 15

Information, training and instruction

Safety representatives and safety committees

Regulations require that employers consult with employees on health and safety matters. The Health and Safety (Consultation with Employees) Regulations 1996 apply to all employees, while the Safety Representatives and Safety Committees Regulations 1977 are applicable to employees who are members of recognised trade unions.

There is evidence from the Trades Union Council that where information is made readily available to people and they are party to the decision-making process regarding the way activities are developed and carried out, the number of accidents that occur is reduced.

We recommend that:
♦ larger voluntary groups should adopt the procedure of establishing a safety committee to oversee health and safety within their organisation;
♦ discussions on matters of health and safety information should be a regular agenda item for your management committee meetings, and any decisions should be minuted and made available to all members.

Generally speaking, the more information on matters of health and safety that are made available to people, the better informed and equipped they are to avoid accidents and to make decisions regarding their health and safety. Don't forget that some people may require information in languages other than English.

By law, employers must display copies of the following:
♦ A current certificate from your insurance company showing that you have employers' liability insurance.[1]
♦ The 'Health & Safety Law' poster for employees.[2] Alternatively, give a leaflet to each individual.
♦ Details of action to be taken in the case of fire, how to raise the alarm, what to do when the alarm is sounded, how to call the fire brigade, the fire escape route, assembly points, emergency exits, fire extinguisher points, fire doors (as designated on the fire certificate).
♦ The location of the first aid point/box, and the name and location of trained first aiders or the appointed person.
♦ A copy of any specific information or posters regarding regulations that apply to your premises where it is a requirement of those regulations to display information, such as the Manual Handling Operations Regulations 1992.

There is also a legal requirement to give people who could be affected by the activities of the organisation access to copies of the health and safety policy.

Information and training

Following assessments, all staff and volunteers must have information and training on the following, as required:
♦ emergency evacuation procedures (including in the event of a fire);

1 *Employers' Liability (Compulsory Insurance) Regulations 1998.*
2 *Poster, 'Health & Safety Law – What you should know' (ISBN 011 7014294)*

♦ accident reporting;
♦ first aid treatment and facilities;
♦ arrangements for the health and safety problems specifically relating to their work, including:
  – rules and regulations, and
  – risk assessments of their workplace.

Note: all HSE publications are available from HMSO bookshops or direct from HSE Books (see appendix 3).

When you have completed this chapter, turn to the checklist on page 65 and tick off the actions you have taken.

Appendix 1
Progress checklist

Chapter	Have you:	Yes	Not applicable	You should enter these into the relevant part of your policy:
2 – Your health and safety policy	• prepared your health and safety policy statement of intent?			**In Part 1** (statement of intent)
	• named the person with overall responsibility?			**In Part 2** (organisation)
3 – Registering your activity	• notified the relevant agency? • applied for any appropriate licence?			**In Part 2** Name the relevant agency and the person who has made the application
4 – Insurance	• insured against identified risks?			**In Part 2** Name of person in organisation responsible for insurance **In Part 3** Details of the insurance cover obtained
5 – Risk assessment	• prepared a list of risks which need assessment and introduced a plan to carry them out?			**In Part 3** The risk assessments and details of the procedures to be followed to eliminate or reduce the risk
6 – Health, safety and welfare	• identified those Acts and Regulations which could apply to your organisation?			**In Part 3** List applicable Acts/Regulations and proposed ways of achieving compliance
7 – CoSHH assessments	• identified substances present which are hazardous?			**In Part 3** The CoSHH assessments and procedures required to control the use of the substances

continued overleaf

Chapter	Have you:	Yes	Not applicable	You should enter these into the relevant part of your policy:
8 – Fire	• applied for fire certificate?			**In Part 3** Details of the restrictions/ requirements of the fire certificate
	• completed fire records and information form?			**In Part 2** The person responsible for ensuring equipment is serviced
	• carried out fire risk assessments?			**In Part 3** Assessments and procedures required to control the risks
	• devised fire and emergency procedures, including training?			**In Part 2** Those persons with responsibilities in the procedures **In Part 3** Details of the fire procedures
9 – Conflict in the workplace	• identified the risks associated with violence and carried out risk assessments?			**In Part 3** Assessments and procedures required to control the risks
10 – Stress	• carried out an assessment to determine levels of stress?			**In Part 3** The assessments and details of the procedures to be followed to prevent or address causes of stress
11 – First aid	• carried out risk assessment to decide first aid requirements?			**In Part 2** Those persons with responsibilities for first aid **In Part 3** Assessments and procedures required to meet the first aid requirements, including training and information
12 – Individuals with specific needs: Young persons	• considered the responsibilities regarding children and young people? • Carried out risk assessments			**In Part 2** Those persons with responsibilities for children and young persons **In Part 3** Assessments and procedures required to control the risks

Chapter	Have you:	Yes	Not applicable	You should enter these into the relevant part of your policy:
13 – Food hygiene	• determined how the legislation relating to food affects your organisation?			**In Part 2** The person responsible for registering food activities to the EHSD **In Part 3** Procedures required to meet the food hygiene requirements, including training and information
14 – Recording and reporting sickness, incidents and accidents	• established your accident reporting and investigation procedure?			**In Part 2** Those persons with responsibilities for accident reporting and retention of personal data which complies with the Data Protection Act and investigation of accidents and incidents. **In Part 3** Systems and procedures required to record and investigate accidents, including training and knowledge of the procedures
15 – Information, training and instruction	• identified the information and training required? • implemented measures to meet those needs?			**In Part 2** Those persons with responsibilities for training and instruction **In Part 3** Training and information which has to be given
From all chapters	• identified legislation which is relevant to your organisation?			**In Part 3** List relevant legislation

Appendix 2
Blank health and safety policy

Health and Safety Policy

PART 1: GENERAL STATEMENT OF POLICY

This document is the health and safety policy of [name of organisation]:

_____

Our policy is to provide healthy and safe working conditions, equipment and systems of work for all our employees, volunteers and members, and to provide all training and information as necessary. We also accept responsibility for all other people who may be affected by our activities.

This policy will be kept up to date, particularly as the organisation changes in nature and size. It will be reviewed at least once a year.

Overall and final responsibility is vested in:

Name _____

Position _____

Date _____

Note: the person named above should be a senior person in your organisation.

Even if the responsibility is delegated to one person, the actual responsibility is shared between all members of the governing body.

Health and Safety Policy
PART 2: ORGANISATION OF HEALTH AND SAFETY

PERSON WITH OVERALL RESPONSIBILITY

The person with overall responsibility for health and safety in this organisation is

_____

REGISTRATION OF THE ACTIVITY [fill in a) or b) as appropriate]

a) The activity was registered with _____ on (date) _____

and form _____ was completed and sent.

Signed _____ Date _____

b) Having contacted _____ on _____

I was informed there is no need to register the activity.

Signed _____ Date _____

If you change your activities, fill in section c)

c) The owner/leaseholder of the property was notified of our activity on _____

Signed _____ Date _____

FIRE PRECAUTIONS

The person with overall responsibility for fire precautions is

_____

If the following tasks are delegated, fill in the names of people given responsibility   Date

a) Initial risk assessment and contact with fire brigade _____ _____

b) Obtaining and organising the maintenance and
   testing of fire equipment and keeping records _____ _____

c) Completing the fire drill procedure _____ _____

d) Compiling the fire notices _____ _____

e) Preparing the emergency evacuation procedure _____ _____

f) Responsible for the fire register _____ _____

g) Making sure the drill is carried out on a regular basis _____ _____

INSURANCE

The person responsible for insuring the activities of the organisation is

_____

FIRST AID

a) The person responsible for first aid assessment in the organisation is

_____

b) The first aider(s) in the organisation is/are _____

_____

RECORDING AND REPORTING OF ACCIDENTS AND INCIDENTS

The person responsible for investigating, recording and reporting accidents and incidents (including violence) is

_____

Health and Safety Policy
PART 3: ARRANGEMENTS AND PROCEDURES

GENERAL FIRE SAFETY

a) Local fire brigade

Contact name _____

Tel. _____

b) Company hired to check, maintain and service fire safety equipment

Company name _____

Address _____

_____

_____

Contact name _____

Tel. _____

c) List of equipment and its location

Item	Location	Service date

d) Fire certificate issued by _____

Renewal date _____

e) Notes _____

_____

_____

_____

_____

_____

Health and Safety Policy
PART 3: ARRANGEMENTS AND PROCEDURES continued

f) Notice of procedure in case of fire

If you discover a fire:

1 Operate the fire alarm without putting yourself in danger

2 Go to your place of assembly at _____

3 Call the fire brigade on 999

On hearing the fire alarm:

1 Leave the building by the quickest available route

2 Go to your place of assembly at _____

Do not leave the assembly point until told to do so by _____

Do not return to the building until told to do so by _____

g) Location of fire exits, extinguishers, escape routes and assembly points (with a map of the premises)

Note: All notices must comply with the Safety Sign Regulations – e.g. 'Must do' signs should be in blue and of a certain size.

Health and Safety Policy
PART 3: ARRANGEMENTS AND PROCEDURES continued

EMPLOYERS' LIABILITY INSURANCE FORM

Name of insurance company _____

Address _____

_____

_____

_____

Tel. _____

Contact name _____

Policy number _____

Date of expiry _____

Amount insured _____

Special exclusions _____

Special conditions _____

PUBLIC LIABILITY INSURANCE FORM

Name of insurance company _____

Address _____

_____

_____

_____

Tel. _____

Contact name _____

Policy number _____

Date of expiry _____

Amount insured _____

Special exclusions _____

Special conditions _____

Health and Safety Policy
PART 3: ARRANGEMENTS AND PROCEDURES continued

SPECIAL RISK INSURANCE

The following items and risks will be insured

_____

_____

_____

_____

DRIVER REGISTRATION FORM

Organisation's name _____

Address _____

_____

_____

Driver's name _____

Age_____ years _____ months

Address _____

_____

_____

Driving licence number_____

Licence checked?   ☐ Yes   ☐ No   Date checked_____

Date passed test _____

Endorsement points_____   Completed minibus test?   ☐ Yes   ☐ No   Date_____

Approved to drive certain vehicles only_____

Medical conditions_____

Checked

☐ medical certificate

☐ occasional cover insurance

☐ appropriate insurance cover

☐ insurance document enclosed?

DECLARATION

The above details are, to the best of my knowledge, complete and accurate

Signed (employee)_____ Date_____

Signed (on behalf of organisation) _____ Date_____

Health and Safety Policy
PART 3: ARRANGEMENTS AND PROCEDURES continued

LIST THE ACTS AND REGULATIONS THAT ARE APPLICABLE TO YOUR ORGANISATION

_____

_____

_____

_____

_____

_____

_____

_____

_____

_____

_____

RISK ASSESSMENT

The following assessments have been carried out

	Yes	N/A	Date
Health and safety			
CoSHH			
Fire			
Violence			
First aid			
Young persons			

Appendix 3
Points of contact for the Health and Safety Executive (HSE)

The way of contacting the HSE will depend on where you work or the information you want.

1 All general enquiries and information

There is a national telephone public enquiry service called HSE Infoline 0845 3450055, open 8am–6pm. Monday to Friday.
Fax: 029 2085 9269; Minicom: 029 2080 8537
E-mail: hseinformationservices@natbrit.com

2 Regional information centres

These are for personal callers who want to consult information held at these centres, which are open 9am to 5pm, Monday to Friday.

London Information Centre
HSE, Rose Court, 2 Southwark Bridge, London SE1 9HS

Bootle Information Centre
HSE, Magdalen House, Trinity Road, Bootle, Merseyside L20 3QZ

Sheffield Information Centre
(*for written or faxed enquiries, as well as personal callers*)
HSE, Broad Lane, Sheffield S3 7HQ
Fax: 0114 289 2333

3 HSE publications

Free leaflets and priced publications can be ordered from HSE Books directly:

HSE Books, PO Box 1999, Sudbury, Suffolk CO10 6FS
Tel: 01787 881165; Fax 01787 313995
E-mail: hsebooks@prolog.uk.com
Website: www.hsebooks.co.uk

4 HSE regional offices

For full, up-to-date details you can contact HSE's online enquiry service
www.hse.gov.uk/contact/ask.htm
or by telephone on 0845 345 0055.

Wales and South West
Covers Wales, Cornwall, Devon, Somerset, North Somerset, Bath and North East Somerset, Gloucestershire, South Gloucestershire, Bristol, Dorset, Swindon and Wiltshire

Government Buildings
Phase 1
Ty Glas
Llanishen
CARDIFF CF14 5SH
Tel: 029 2026 3000
Fax: 029 2026 3120

Covers: Merthyr Tydfil, Rhondda Cynon Taff, Vale of Glamorgan, Bridgend, Neath, Port Talbot, Powys, Blaenau Gwent, Caerphilly, Cardiff, Monmouthshire, Newport Torfaen and part of Powys

4th Floor, The Pithay
All Saints Street
BRISTOL BS1 2ND
Tel: 01179 886000
Fax: 01179 262998

Covers: Bristol, Somerset, Bath and North East Somerset, North Somerset, Gloucestershire, South Gloucestershire, Dorset (public services only), Swindon and Wiltshire
Agriculture in North, Mid and East Devon

Construction in Devon (but not Cornwall or Plymouth City Council area – see Plymouth Office)

Ballard House
West Hoe Road
PLYMOUTH PL1 3BL
Tel: 01752 276300
Fax: 01752 226024

Covers: Devon, Cornwall (all industries except public services and quarries)
Agriculture except in North, Mid and East Devon
Construction (all of Cornwall plus Plymouth City Council area, rest of Devon – see Bristol Office)
Unit 7 & 8 Edison Court
Ellice Way

Wrexham Technology Park
Wrexham
CLWYD LL13 7YT
Tel: 01978 316000
Fax: 01978 355669

Covers: Anglesey, Conwy, Denbighshire, Flintshire, Wrexham, Gwynedd and part of Powys

3rd Floor
Darkgate Buildings
3 Red Street
Carmarthen
DYFED SA31 1QL
Tel: 01267 244230
Fax: 01267 223267

Covers: Carmarthenshire, Pembrokeshire, Ceredigion and Swansea

14 New Fields
Stinsford Road
Nuffield Industrial Estate
Poole
DORSET BH17 0NF
Tel: 01202 634400
Fax: 01202 667224

Covers: Dorset (except public services – covered by Bristol)

East and South East
Covers the counties of Bedfordshire, Berkshire, Buckinghamshire, Cambridgeshire, Essex, Hampshire, Hertfordshire, Isle of Wight, Norfolk, Suffolk, Oxfordshire, Kent, East & West Sussex and Surrey

14 Cardiff Road
LUTON
LU1 1PP
Tel: 01582 444200
Fax: 01582 444320

Covers: Bedfordshire, Hertfordshire, Cambridge, (Buckinghamshire – construction only, all other Bucks enquiries to Basingstoke)

Priestley House
Priestley Road
BASINGSTOKE
RG24 9NW
Tel: 01256 404000
Fax: 01256 404100

Covers: Hampshire, Berkshire, Isle of Wight, Oxfordshire, and Buckinghamshire except for construction-related enquiries as these should be referred to Luton

Wren House
Hedgerows Business Park
Colchester Road
Springfield
CHELMSFORD
CM2 5PF
Tel: 01245 706200
Fax: 01245 706222

Covers: Essex (except Barking, Redbridge and Waltham Forest – these LAs are covered by London), Norfolk and Suffolk
See also Norwich Office

Phoenix House
23–25 Cantelupe Road
EAST GRINSTEAD
West Sussex
RH19 3BE
Tel: 01342 334200
Fax: 01342 334222

Covers: Kent (service industries only), East & West Sussex, Surrey

Kiln House
Pottergate
Norwich
NORFOLK NR2 1DA
Tel: 01603 753800
Fax: 01603 761436

Covers: Norfolk, Suffolk, Essex (please also see Chelmsford)

International House
Dover Place
Ashford
KENT TN23 1HU
Tel: 01233 653900
Fax: 01233 634827

Covers: Kent (except service industries – as these enquiries should be direct to East Grinstead)

London
Rose Court
2 Southwark Bridge
LONDON
SE1 9HS
Tel: 020 7556 2100
Fax: 020 7556 2102

Covers: London only

Midlands
Covers the counties of West Midlands, Leicestershire, Northamptonshire, Warwickshire, Derbyshire, Lincolnshire, Nottinghamshire, Herefod and Worcester

1 Hagley Road
BIRMINGHAM
B16 8HS
Tel: 0121 607 6200
Fax: 0120 607 6349

Covers: West Midlands and Warwickshire

5th Floor Belgrave House
1 Greyfriars
NORTHAMPTON
NN1 2BS
Tel: 01604 738300
Fax: 01604 738333

Covers: Northampton, Leicestershire, Rutland

1st Floor
The Pearson Building
55 Upper Parliament Street
NOTTINGHAM
NG1 6AU
Tel: 01159 712800
Fax: 01159 712802

Covers: Nottinghamshire, Derbyshire, Lincolnshire (most) (North Lincolnshire covered by Sheffield office)

The Marches House
Midway
NEWCASTLE-UNDER-LYME
ST5 1DT
Tel: 01782 602300
Fax: 01782 602400

Covers: Staffordshire and Shropshire

National Agricultural Centre
Stoneleigh
Kenilworth
WARWICKSHIRE CV8 2LG
Tel: 02476 698350
Fax: 02476 696542

Covers: Warwickshire, West Mids, Leicestershire

Haswell House
St Nicholas Street
WORCESTER
WR1 1UW
Tel: 01905 743600
Fax: 01905 723045

Covers: Worcestershire and Herefordshire

Health and Safety Laboratory
Harpur Hill
Buxton
Derbyshire
SK17 9JN
Tel: 01298 218000
Fax: 01298 218590

Yorkshire and North East
Covers the counties of Cleveland, Durham, North Yorkshire, Northumberland, West Yorkshire, Tyne & Wear, Humberside and South Yorkshire.

Marshalls Mill
Marshall Street
LEEDS
LS11 9YJ
Tel: 0113 283 4200
Fax No: 0113 283 4383 (general enquiries)
Fax No: 0113 283 4296 (completed F10 forms)

Covers: West and North Yorkshire

Edgar Allen House
241 Glossop Road
SHEFFIELD
S10 2GW
Tel: 0114 291 2300
Fax: 0114 291 2379

Covers: East Yorkshire, North Lincolnshire, NE Lincolnshire, South Yorkshire, Kingston-upon-Hull

Arden House
Regent Centre
Regent Farm Road
Gosforth
NEWCASTLE-UPON-TYNE NE3 3JN
Tel: 0191 202 6200
Fax: 0191 202 6300

Covers: Northumberland, Tyne and Wear, Durham, Cleveland

North West
Covers the counties of Cheshire, Cumbria, Greater Manchester, Lancashire and Merseyside

Grove House
Skerton Road
MANCHESTER
M16 0RB
Tel: 0161 952 8200
Fax: 0161 952 8222

Covers: Merseyside, Cheshire, Greater Manchester

Marshall House
Ringway
PRESTON
PR1 2HS
Tel: 0161 952 8200
Fax: 01772 836 222

Covers: Lancashire, Cumbria

2 Victoria Place
CARLISLE CA1 1ER
Tel: 01228 634100
Fax: 01228 548482

Covers: Cumbria (except services, metals & minerals and fairgrounds)

Bootle Headquarters
Daniel House, Trinity Road, Bootle, Merseyside, L20 3TW
Magdalen House, Stanley Precinct, Bootle, Merseyside, L20 3QZ
Merton House, Stanley Road, Bootle, Merseyside, L20 3DL
St Anne's House, Stanley Precinct, Bootle, Merseyside, L20 3RA
St Hugh's House, Stanley Precinct, Bootle, Merseyside, L20 3QY
St Peter's House, Stanley Precinct, Bootle, Merseyside, L20 3JZ

Scotland
Covers all the Scottish unitary authorities and island councils

Belford House
59 Belford Road
EDINBURGH
EH4 3UE
Tel: 0131 247 2000
Fax: 0131 247

Covers: Borders, Lothian, Central Park, Kinross, Fife and Dundee

375 West George Street
GLASGOW
G2 4LW
Tel: 0141 275 3000
Fax: 0141 275 3100

Covers: West Scotland

Lord Cullen House
Fraser Place
ABERDEEN AB25 3UB
Tel: 01224 252500
Fax: 01224 252525

Covers: Angus, Aberdeenshire, Moray and Shetland

Offshore Safety Division
Lord Cullen House
Fraser Place
ABERDEEN AB25 3UB
Tel: 01224 252500
Fax: 01224 252662

Covers: Aberdeen

Longman House
28 Lonman Road
Longman Industrial Estate
INVERNESS IV1 1SF
Tel: 01463 723260
Fax: 001463 713458

Covers: Highlands and Orkney

Construction Division
Covers: London Division, East and South East, Midlands, Wales and South West, Yorkshire & North East Division, North West Division and Scotland

Rose Court
2 Southwark Bridge
LONDON
SE1 9HS
Tel: 020 7556 2100
Fax: 020 7556 2109

Appendix 4
Legislation

Statutes

Charities Act 1993

Child Protection Act 1990

Children's Act 1989

Disability Discrimination Act 1995

Factories Act 1961

Fire Precautions Act 1971

Food Safety Act 1990

Health and Safety at Work etc. Act 1974

Occupiers Liability Acts 1957 and 1984

Offices, Shops and Railway Premises Act 1963

Regulations

Chemicals (Hazard Information and Packaging for Supply) Regulations 1994 (CHIP 2)

Construction (Design & Management) Regulations 1994

Control of Substances Hazardous to Health (CoSHH) Regulations 1994

Disability Discrimination (Employment) Regulations 1996

Electricity at Work Regulations 1989

Employers' Liability (Compulsory Insurance) Regulations 1998

Employers' Liability (Compulsory Insurance) Regulations General (Amendment) Regulations 1994

Fire Precautions (Workplace) Regulations 1997

Fire Precautions (Workplace) (Amendment) Regulations 1999

Food Premises (Registration) Regulations 1991

Food Safety (General Food Hygiene) Regulations 1995

Food Safety (Temperature Control) Regulations 1995

Gas Safety (Installation & Use) Regulations 1994

Health and Safety (Consultation with Employees) Regulations 1996

Health and Safety (Display Screen Equipment) Regulations 1992

Health and Safety (First Aid) Regulations 1981

Health and Safety (Safety Signs and Signals) Regulations 1996

Health and Safety (Training for Work) Regulations 1990

Highly Flammable Liquids and Petroleum Gases Regulations 1972

Management of Health and Safety at Work Regulations 1999

Manual Handling Operations Regulations 1992

Noise at Work Regulations 1989

Personal Protective Equipment at Work Regulations 1992

Provision and Use of Work Equipment Regulations 1998

Reporting of Injuries, Diseases and Dangerous Occurrences Regulations 1995 (RIDDOR)

Safety Representatives and Safety Committees Regulations 1977

Workplace (Health, Safety and Welfare) Regulations 1992